AFTER-SCHOOL EXPLORATIONS

Fun, Ready-to-Use Activities for Kids Ages 5-12

Susanna Palomares ♦ Dianne Schilling

Cover: Dave Cowan

Artwork: Linda Thille

Copyright © 2012 by Innerchoice Publishing • All rights reserved

ISBN - 10: 1-56499-081-8

ISBN - 13: 978-1-56499-081-5

INNERCHOICE Publishing
15079 Oak Chase Court
Wellington, FL 33414

www.InnerchoicePublishing.com

Contents

Solving Problems and Making Decisions   87

My Health and Safety   99

Caring for the Environment   121

Introduction

The best after-school programs provide a balance of academic, recreation, enrichment, and cultural activities. After-school is not an extension of the school day but rather an extra-curricula experience that combines fun and learning. *"After-School Explorations"* is designed to help meet the programming needs of a diverse group of children by providing engaging, academically enriching, hands-on learning experiences that are easy to implement and fun to do. The activities in this book address the multi-dimensional needs of children ages 5 to 12 by encouraging them to interact with others while involving their own intuition, emotions, talents, interests, and sensitivities.

The children in your after-school program have already been through six hours of schooling and it's unrealistic to expect them to "sit up straight and listen quietly" when they get to after-school. The activities in this book promote both play and playfulness while still providing important learning opportunities. After-school is the perfect place to demonstrate that academic enrichment can be enjoyable for children!

After-School Explorations provides activities that will help your children engage their problem-solving abilities and relationship skills to learn new abilities and understand new concepts. Through the lessons provided, children get to experiment and explore. Movement is encouraged, and learning is always active, never passive. Through engagement with others, and active, playful involvement of the emotional centers of the brain, truly the doors to learning are activated, and thereby promote higher levels of creativity and cognition.

A balanced program where children learn through multi-sensory experiences and play reaches more children at more levels targets the full spectrum of intelligences and achieves greater relevance and self-esteem in the process.

Seven Areas of Focus

The activities in *After-School Explorations* are grouped into seven developmental areas, but are not otherwise sequential. Each activity stands alone and may be implemented in whatever order makes sense to you. The goal is to develop in children positive perceptions of themselves and their place in the world. The areas of focus are arranged in a logical order progressing from a focus on "Me" to a concern for "My world." The following overviews will give you some idea what to expect as you delve into the choices.

Learning About Me

Activities in this unit are designed to help children develop greater awareness of themselves and their peers including physical characteristics and growth rates, similarities and differences, likes and dislikes, favored activities, achievements, and emotions. The children observe, describe, measure, and compare. They participate in movement, writing, and art activities, and they give and receive esteem-enhancing recognition and affirmation throughout.

Living with My Family and Community

This group of activities focuses on the close connections children have with family, school, after-school personnel, and vital members of the immediate community. The children explore family roles, responsibilities, composition, and history; recreate home-based activities through play; learn about supportive enterprises in the neighborhood and community; and contribute tangibly to the smooth functioning of the these environments.

Communicating with Others

It's never too early to foster effective communication skills. In these activities children learn to identify and discriminate among various sounds; follow precise instructions in game-like settings; practice good listening and clear, accurate expression; and communicate in writing.

Cooperating with Others

These activities focus on friendship skills and the kinds of cooperative, collaborative behaviors needed to accomplish group tasks and projects. The children participate in movement, writing, art, and planning activities in small groups, experience the importance of rules and following directions, and share the benefits of their cooperative endeavors.

Solving Problems and Making Decisions

All children can learn the basics of good decision making and problem solving. These activities present simple processes for both and give children plenty of enjoyable practice in the use of these models. Emphasis is placed on safe versus unsafe decisions and on seeking adult counsel in doubtful situations.

My Health and Safety

Through simple science experiments and experiential activities, these lessons cover a wide range of health habits and safety practices. Hand-washing, avoiding hazardous products, handling emergencies, traffic safety, understanding signage, and knowing basic family information are just a few of the topics.

Caring for the Environment

In this unit, the children participate in a variety of activities involving plants, trees, birds, habitats, air currents, composting, recycling, conservation, and litter abatement. They explore a variety of environmental topics and become more aware of and sensitive to the natural world in which they live. Nearly all of the activities are experiential and promote cooperative learning.

Using the Activities

As you implement the lessons in *After-School Explorations*, feel free to modify the activities to suit the maturity, reading ability, culture, and interests of your children. Apply your own expertise as well. Enhancements based on your knowledge and experience are welcomed and encouraged.

The level of difficulty among the activities may vary slightly. If you like an activity, but think that the presentation is too sophisticated (or too simple) for your children, look for ways to modify it. Change the vocabulary, revise the explanations, and give examples that the children will find familiar.

We recommend that you integrate the activities within your after-school program, adding them wherever they seem appropriate. Since most of the activities are experiential and dynamic, they provide welcome breaks from more sedentary tasks and school-day activities, such as reading, testing, and computing. Giving the children chances to move around and work in cooperative teams will also improve their concentration when it's time for them to return to more solitary work.

Many of the activities call for the use of supporting skills, such as listening, decision making, and problem solving. Some involve the use of math skills, reading and writing skills, and social studies concepts. Enough information is always provided to allow for smooth implementation of the activity; however, you may want to take advantage of such opportunities to expand the lessons and present additional material.

After Play, Discussion

At the conclusion of every activity in this collection, you will find a list of discussion questions. Discussion questions are provided to help you involve children in thinking about and summarizing what they have experienced and learned from a particular activity. Discussion assures a conclusion that is more roundly cognitive, during which the children have an opportunity to consciously weave together the concepts they've learned and integrate the various aspects of an experience.

Discussion promotes thoughtful reasoning, the use of higher-level thinking skills, and internalization of knowledge and skills. It meets the need of youngsters of all ages to find greater meaning in what they do. When planning for implementation, always allow plenty of time for discussion.

Discussion doesn't always have to come at the end of an activity. For example, when children are sharing their creations following an art activity, discussion questions can be asked of the entire group at appropriate moments during the sharing process. Questions can also be asked as you circulate and assist the children with the creative process itself. Familiarize yourself with the questions in advance and then ask them at teachable moments throughout the experience. Encourage the children to ask questions, too. Invite them to challenge one another's thinking and yours.

If the discussion questions that are provided don't seem particularly relevant to what the children are experiencing, by all means come up with some of your own. You may want to ask questions that relate back to an earlier lesson or activity, or to some other experience the children are having. You have knowledge about the lives of your children outside the after-school that can open up endless opportunities to make connections and promote relevance. We encourage you to use those opportunities liberally and wisely.

Many of the activities in *After-School Explorations* will open avenues to new areas of interest. Notice sparks of enthusiasm and curiosity, and expand learning in these areas by developing additional activities, reading related literature, performing role plays, creating works of art, and visiting places in the community. The possibilities in any area are virtually endless. Above all, let the children experience and enjoy, and trust that learning will follow.

Learning About Me

8

The Magic Chair

Receiving honest, positive feedback from others is one way children develop a positive self-image. Through this activity, the children receive positive feedback from one another when they sit in the "magic" chair.

Objectives

The children will:
- give and receive positive feedback.
- develop enhanced self-images.

Materials

decorative materials and a chair

Procedure

Select a spare chair that can be used as the Magic Chair. Decorate it in a fashion that renders it regal-looking and desirable. For example, cover it with gold fabric, silver foil, or a fake fur throw. Tape a sign reading "Magic Chair" to the back of the chair.

Tell the children that when they sit in the Magic Chair, they will hear lots of wonderful and positive things about themselves.

Ask the class to sit in a semicircle on the floor in front of the chair. Invite a child to sit in the chair. Go around the circle and ask one child at a time to say something nice to the child in the chair—a positive observation, an admired trait, or an attractive feature. Make the first comment yourself to model the process.

Allow two or three children to sit in the chair each day. To avoid rote responses and excessive repetition, don't feature too many children per day.

Discussion Questions

1. What is magic about the Magic Chair?
2. How do you feel when you sit in the Magic Chair?
3. Why is it important to say positive things to each other?
4. What would our group be like if we didn't value and appreciate one another?

Measuring Our Growth

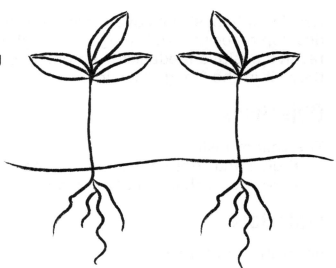

This is a year-long growth monitoring activity that works best if initiated at the beginning of the year. Throughout the year, as children measure their growth, they are learning to recognize, respect, and appreciate individual differences. This experience ends with a math activity.

Objectives

The children will:
- recognize and acknowledge the physical growth of themselves and others.
- learn record-keeping and measurement methods.

Materials

a 5-foot length of sturdy paper (such as butcher paper), chart paper, crayons or colored marking pens

Procedure

Tape a 5-foot length of paper vertically to a wall or door. Have each child stand in stocking feet with his or her back against the paper. Mark the date, and the child's name and height, on the paper. Repeat this measuring routine every two months throughout the year. (When new children join the class, add them to the chart.)

At the end of the year, after you have measured the growth of the children several times, create a chart depicting the results. On a large sheet of chart paper, draw a vertical column for each child, plus one extra column on the left side of the chart.

In the (extra) column on the left, mark off feet and inches.

As you read off each series of recorded measurements, have one child at a time fill in his or her column up to the point of the first height measurement with one color (e.g., to 3 feet, 8 inches), up to the point of the second measurement with a second color (e.g., from 3 feet, 8 inches to 3 feet, 9 1/2 inches), up to the point of the third measurement with a third color (e.g., from 3 feet, 9 1/2 inches to 3 feet, 11 inches), and so on. Include a final measurement of the child's current height, which can be taken that day.

Take a few minutes to look at the completed chart with the children. Have the children use simple subtraction to determine how much they grew during each interval.

Compare growth patterns and discuss the subject of physical growth.

Discussion Questions

1. Which three children grew the most from the beginning of the year until now?
2. Which three grew the least?
3. Why do we grow at different rates?
4. Did you grow more at the beginning of the year, the middle of the year, or the end of the year?
5. How can you take care of yourself every day to ensure the best growth possible for you?

Birthday Acknowledgments

In this year-long activity, mini-posters featuring individual children are displayed during their birthday months. Birthdays are extra-special days and provide a perfect way to acknowledge a child and affirm his or her sense of self-worth. This kind of positive attention can go far to increase children's feelings of esteem and value, and is well worth the time.

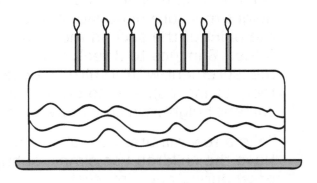

Objectives

The children will:
- recognize the birthdays of classmates.
- acknowledge and appreciate one another's unique qualities.

Materials

computer, printer, and graphics software; or construction paper, colored marking pens, and glue; a digital or printed photograph of each child either contributed by the child or taken during class with a digital camera

Procedure

At the beginning of the year, develop a list of the children and their birthdays, organized by month. Create a mini-poster for each child whose birthday falls during the current month. Create mini-posters for succeeding months a few at a time, staying at least one month ahead of the date they will be needed.

Make computer-generated mini-posters the size of a regular sheet of paper (8.5 × 11), or allow two posters per sheet if you wish to conserve space and supplies. Make hand-drawn posters any uniform size that is easily visible when displayed on a bulletin board.

In large letters, write the name and birth date of the child. In smaller letters, list two or three positive statements about the child. For example, list physical characteristics (Jesse has big brown eyes), favorite activities (Lisa likes to read), or positive qualities (Marty is friendly).

Attach or import a photograph of the child. Embellish the mini-poster with a frame and other appropriate graphic elements.

To help keep this on-going experience organized arrange your hand-drawn mini-posters in chronological order in a box. Store digital posters in monthly files on the computer and print them out as needed.

Post each child's mini-poster on the bulletin board during his or her birthday month. Acknowledge children whose birthdays fall during vacation months by posting them during the preceding month.

Hold a special celebration each month for the featured children. Discuss how they contribute to the class, drawing attention to their special qualities.

Discussion Questions

1. Why do we celebrate birthdays?
2. What have you learned about the children whose birthdays we are celebrating this month?
3. How does getting to know each other help make this a better class?
4. How do we show people that we think they have special qualities?
5. What would happen if all people had exactly the same special qualities?

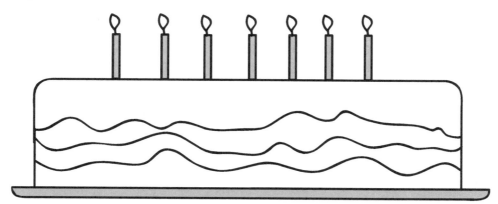

Photos of Us

Photos of the children are taken and displayed around the room to enjoy and to stimulate discussion concerning physical characteristics. This is another activity which encourages the children to recognize, accept, respect, and appreciate individual differences while also acknowledging the uniqueness of each individual child.

Objectives

The children will:
- name physical characteristics that they have in common.
- recognize unique physical features in themselves and others.
- recognize and appreciate characteristics that all humans have in common.

Materials

digital camera; construction paper or lightweight poster board, colored marking pens, and spray mount or glue

Procedure

Tell the children that you are going to take photos of them and that you would like each of them to select a special place for the picture to be taken. Explain that the setting for the photo can be either indoors or outdoors. Urge them to think carefully before selecting the perfect spot for their picture.

With a digital camera, you can take multiple photos of each child and check them for quality immediately, selecting the best one and discarding the rest. Print out copies of the photos.

Mount each photo on a small sheet of construction paper or lightweight poster board, leaving margins all around for the children to embellish with marking pens. Have them sign their photos along the bottom margin, providing assistance to young children who need it.

Display the mounted photographs around the room. Look at the pictures with the children and discuss any similarities and differences they observe in the pictures. List the children's observations on the board or chart paper.

Have the children stand in a large circle facing one another while you lead a culminating discussion. Use the discussion to help the children sharpen their awareness of physical characteristics that people have in common.

When you take down the photo display, place the photos inside protective sheets in a three-ring binder so that the children can continue to enjoy them throughout the year. At the end of the year, send the pictures home with the children..

Discussion Questions

1. Who in the room looks exactly like you?
2. In what ways is every person you see just like you?
3. In what ways are we all different?
4. Which children are the same height as you are? Which have the same color hair?

My Likes and Dislikes

In this self-awareness activity the children construct banners that convey some of their likes and dislikes. As they share and listen, they are also learning to recognize and respect differences in all people.

Objectives

The children will:
- identify and describe specific likes and dislikes.
- learn the likes and dislikes of their classmates.

Materials

construction paper (preferably in light colors), straws, tape, and colored marking pens

Procedure

Begin by facilitating a discussion about things that the children like and dislike. Encourage the children to think of activities they like to do, foods they enjoy eating, holidays they look forward to, and places they like to go. Things they dislike might include chores, specific animals or insects, incidents that lead to trouble, certain times of the day, or days of the year, etc. Accept all comments without judgment.

Announce that the children are going to make banners that show some of the things they like and dislike.

Distribute the art materials. Demonstrate how to make a banner by gluing or taping a piece of construction paper around one end of a straw. Then help the children each make two banners.

Have the children write "Yes!" across the top of one banner and "No!" across the top of the other. Have them write the names of things they like on the Yes! banner and the names of things they dislike on the No! banner. Demonstrate this process on your own sample banner. Use different colors and draw a frame around each listed item so that it stands out from the others. Have young children draw pictures of their likes and dislikes.

Circulate and assist while the children complete their banners.

Play a simple polling game with the banners: Ask one child to hold up his or her Yes! banner and read the names of the items listed. As each item is named, ask the rest of the class to:, "Hold up your banner if you, too, listed ("candy") on your banner." Call on several children in this manner and poll the class to see how many other children listed the same items.

Discussion Questions

1. How do we learn to like things?
2. What caused you to dislike one of the items listed on your banner?
3. What dislike was listed on the most banners?
4. What like was listed on the most banners?
5. Is it possible to dislike something that you know nothing about?

Performing Shadows

Through this movement activity, the children learn about their bodies, and how they move and use them, by experimenting with and controlling their shadows during a series of movement activities.

Objectives

The children will:
- increase their awareness of a variety of body movements.
- use concentrated muscle control to perform specific movements.

Materials

spotlight or other source of strong light for casting shadows

Procedure

Set up the light source so that it casts shadows against a blank wall. Allow plenty of "performing" space between the light source and the wall.

Ask the children to think about the motions their bodies make when they run, walk, throw, wave, jump, leap, hop, bend, stretch in different directions, and perform other actions. Encourage them to try some of the actions while standing in place.

Have the children take turns performing various movements in front of the light source, so that their shadows are cast against the blank wall. Describe actions involving different parts of the body while the children perform those actions. Start by having them reach to the side with one arm, bend their elbow, wave, etc. Then progress to more complex movements. Have the children do each movement twice, first facing the wall and then in profile.

Take suggestions for additional movements from the class.

Discussion Questions

1. What was the most difficult movement you tried? What made it tough?
2. Which movements looked different than you expected them to?
3. What does it mean to exaggerate a movement?
4. Did you exaggerate the movements a lot or a little? Why?
5. What did you learn about controlling your body from this activity?

Face Paintings

This is a classic face-painting activity with a language arts twist. If the children are not mature enough to paint each other's faces, save this activity for a day when two or three parent volunteers can act as face-painting artists.

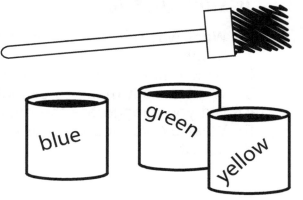

Objectives

The children will:
- choose characters to "become" for a day or part of a day.
- create and share stories about their characters.

Materials

petroleum jelly and food coloring in several colors, or watercolor paints and water; assorted brushes; photos or drawings of animals, clowns, and other characters for the artists to copy (optional)

Procedure

Make the face paints by mixing a few drops of food coloring into a small amount of petroleum jelly, or by adding a few drops of water to watercolor paints. Set out the paints and brushes at work stations.

If the children are mature enough, have them form pairs and paint each other's faces. If not, have them take turns getting their faces painted by a parent volunteer. Allow each child to choose the character he or she would like to be (cat, dog, zebra, bird, pig, squirrel, clown, old person, etc.).

After all of the faces have been painted, have the children sit in a circle and take turns telling the class something about their characters. Encourage them to give their characters names and to use their imaginations to create stories about them. As an alternative, have the children write stories about their characters and then share them with the class.

Learning About Me

Try having the children spend the entire after-school session "in character." At the end of the time, ask the children what it was like to experience the world as someone or something else for an entire school day.

Discussion Questions

1. How do you feel as a (cat, dog, clown, etc.)?
2. What does your character like to do all day?
3. What kind of family does your character have?
4. Where does your character live?
5. Is it easy or hard to stay in character?
6. How is your character like the real you? How is it different?

Look at Me! Look at You!

A mirror is used as the focal point of this self-awareness activity in which the children hone their observational skills and are helped to recognize their own uniqueness that make them special and one of a kind.

Objectives

The children will:
- practice visual observation skills.
- give and receive positive feedback.
- gain awareness of the physical impression they make on others.

Materials

full-length mirror, art materials

Procedure

Place the mirror in the front of the room or in some other location where the children can gather around it. Talk about the usefulness of mirrors for checking our appearance, combing our hair, brushing our teeth, judging the fit of an article of clothing, and seeing how well different colors and styles go together.

Have a volunteer stand before the mirror, turn around slowly and study his or her reflection from all sides. Ask the class to think of as many ways as possible to describe how the mirrored child looks. For example:

"Jane has a happy smile."
"Manuel has wavy black hair."
"Ella is wearing a green shirt."
"Maria looks embarrassed."

Use the exercise as an opportunity to compliment the children, to encourage good grooming, and to point out similarities and differences among children. Make sure that every child has an opportunity to take a turn before the mirror and receives positive feedback of some kind. Do not allow put-downs or negative comments.

Distribute the art materials and have the children draw self-portraits based on what they observed in the mirror and on the feedback they received from the other children. Allow them to use the mirror as often as necessary during this process to enhance the accuracy of their likenesses.

When the portraits are finished, ask the children to recall the positive statements made about them during the mirror exercise. Assist them, as necessary, to write one of these statements across the top or bottom of their self-portraits. Display the self-portraits around the room.

Discussion Questions

1. How would you feel if suddenly there weren't any mirrors and you couldn't see yourself except in photographs?
2. What is the difference between just looking at something and really observing it?
3. What did you learn about your own appearance from this exercise?
4. What can you tell about a person's mood by looking at him or her?
5. What can you tell about a person's likes and dislikes by looking at him or her?
6. What was the hardest part about doing a self-portrait? What was the easiest part?

A Game of Communicating Feelings

This feelings-pantomime game helps children develop an understanding of the roles of body language and facial expression in communication.

Objectives

The children will:
- demonstrate a variety of feelings using facial expressions and body language.
- practice identifying feelings based on nonverbal communication.
- understand how nonverbal behaviors contribute to effective communication.

Materials

index cards, marking pen, and a small box to hold the index cards

Procedure

Using the "Feeling Words" list provided, or a list of your own, print one feeling word on each index card. Place the index cards into a box.

Either one at a time or in pairs, have the children reach into the box and draw one feeling-word card. Caution them not to tell the rest of the class which card they selected. After all of the children (or pairs) have a card, direct them to take a few minutes to create a pantomime demonstrating their feeling word. Explain that they are to act out the word with their bodies and faces; they may not say words or make noises. Circulate and provide assistance and encouragement.

Have the children perform their pantomimes for the rest of the class. After the class has shown its appreciation with applause, ask the children to guess the feeling that was demonstrated in each pantomime. If they have difficulty, have the performing group provide hints.

Facilitate discussion between performances.

Discussion Questions

1. How can you tell when someone is angry at you?
2. What kinds of facial expressions show joy? Fear? Doubt?
3. How does feeling sad affect the way you sit and walk?
4. What does it mean to "read" someone's feelings?
5. Who understands your feelings better than anyone? How do they do it?

Feeling Words

happy	naughty	friendly
jealous	proud	beautiful
warm	lazy	angry
brave	guilty	left out
scared	confused	comfortable
loving	lonely	sad
homesick	sick	peaceful
nervous	afraid	ignored
shy	relaxed	tired
powerful	stupid	sleepy
silly	worried	grumpy
excited	hungry	embarrassed

The Wishing Well

Through this activity, the children clarify their desires by writing them on paper coins and tossing the coins into a "wishing well". By them discussing some of the factors involved in making wishes come true, they learn the importance of goal setting and follow-through actions.

Objectives

The children will:
- discuss how wishes come true.
- describe one thing that they want to have, do, or be.

Materials

one copy of the wishing well and multiple copies of the coins (templates provided), tape, writing implements

Procedure

Cut out the wishing well and tape the ends together to form a free-standing circular well. Cut out the coins, making enough to supply the entire group and have several left over.

Ask the children if they have ever made a wish before throwing a coin into a wishing well, or a fountain. Talk about this custom, allowing the children to share their experiences. Ask each volunteer if his or her wish came true and, if so, how the wish was granted. Ask:

Did it just happen?
Did a parent or other adult provide it?
Did you plan and work for it yourself?

In your own words, explain: Making wishes helps us to clarify the things we want to have, do, or be in our lives. And knowing what we want is the first step to achieving it.

Show the children the wishing well and explain that every person in the class is going to have a chance to make a wish and throw a coin into the well. Give one coin to each child and instruct the children to write the name of something they wish for on the coin. Have pre-writers dictate their wishes to you or another adult.

One at a time, have the children put their coins into the wishing well while explaining to the class what they wished for. Place a container of additional coins near the well so that when the children think of other wishes they may drop additional coins into the well. Be sure to take a turn yourself.

Discussion Questions

1. Which wishes can you help your classmates to achieve?
2. What can you do to help your own wish come true?
3. Does it help to wish for a good grade? What can you do?
4. Does wishing for more friends help you make them? What does help?
5. What kinds of things have you achieved by just wishing?

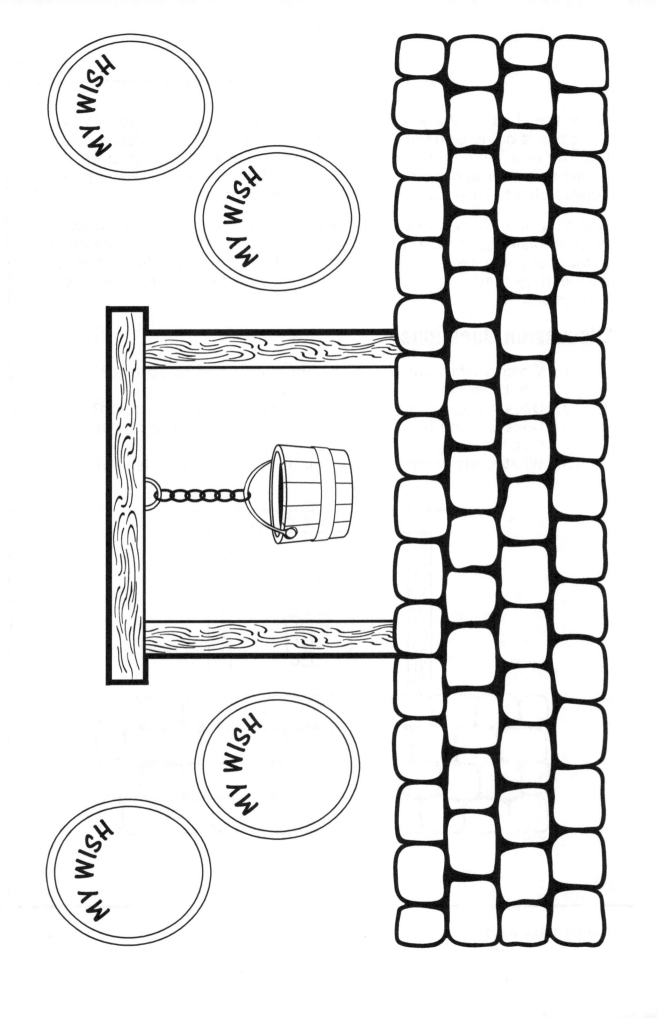

Living with My Family and Community

Playing House

Simple, free play is recognized as a very important part of social and emotional growth as well as intellectual development. In this activity the children create make-believe houses out of packing boxes and use them for creative play.

Objectives

The children will:
- identify activities that are typically done at home.
- dramatize typical household activities in play houses of their own creation.

Materials

several large cardboard packing boxes (e.g., large appliance boxes, moving-company boxes), box cutters or scissors, colored marking pens or paints, carpet samples, fabric remnants, posters, and other decorative materials

Procedure

Use the packing boxes to simulate cozy "houses" by cutting out windows and doors. Have the children decorate with posters, rugs, curtains, and other details drawn on the interior and exterior walls.

Brainstorm a list of the activities that go on in the children's homes (the real ones). For example, cooking, eating, cleaning, watching TV, working on projects, playing alone and with others, caring for pets, homework, reading, etc. When you have a nice long list, post it where the children can see it.

Encourage the children to dramatize these activities while playing in their cardboard houses.

Discussion Questions

1. What do you like best about playing house?
2. What roles have you taken while playing house?
3. What are some important things families do together at home?
4. What problems have you solved in your make-believe house?

My Family

In this activity the children draw family portraits, identifying the contributions of each family member. Knowing how individuals cooperate and contribute to the family helps children develop a sense of belonging and esteem

Objectives

The children will:
- identify family members by name, age, and role.
- describe how each member contributes to the functioning of the family.

Materials

construction or drawing paper, crayons, or colored marking pens

Procedure

Ask the children to indicate the number of people in their immediate family (those living in the home) by holding up the appropriate number of fingers. Talk about the importance of families. Ask volunteers to describe some of the benefits that families provide their members (look after and help support each other, celebrate holidays and birthdays together, offer comfort in times of distress, help in solving problems, etc.).

If the children can write, have them list the members of their immediate families on sheets of paper. Ask the children to identify the various family members by name, age and relationship (e.g., brother). If you have children who are not yet writing, ask them to verbally give you the information and write it down for them.

Distribute the drawing materials and explain the assignment:

Draw a picture showing your entire family. Include everyone on your list, plus yourself. After you have finished the drawing, write a short caption beneath each family member's likeness, naming specific ways in which that person contributes to the household. For example, maybe your sister washes the dishes and your mother earns money by working in an office. Who cooks the meals, feeds the pets, does the shopping, and helps with homework? List as many contributions as you can think of for each person. If you run out of room, turn your drawing over and use the other side.

Circulate and assist any children who have difficulty identifying contributions or writing them down. Young children can represent their ideas with additional small drawings

Display the drawings around the room. In the next activity, the children will share facts and observations about their drawings.

Discussion Questions

1. Which family members were easiest to draw? Which were hardest? Why?
2. How many different contributions were you able to think of?
3. Who has the most responsibilities in your family? Who has the least?
4. How many responsibilities that you listed are shared by more than one person?
5. Why do families need to work cooperatively to get things done?

Families Are Different

After examining the family portraits created in the previous activity, the children help construct a bar chart illustrating family differences. This helps the children recognize and respect differences in various family configurations.

Objectives

The children will:
- identify ways in which their families differ.
- compute differences in specific categories.
- represent family demographics on a bar chart.

Materials

the family portraits from the previous activity

Procedure

Lead the children in a viewing of the family portraits from the previous activity. As you look at each portrait, have the children count the number of family members. Then compare the size and composition of that family with those viewed previously. Ask the children to name ways in which the families differ. For example, some have one parent while others have two, some include a grandparent or other adult, and the number, gender, and ages of the children vary from family to family. Other differences may include skin color, attire, and the presence or absence of pets.

Ask the children to help you make a bar chart showing some of the main ways in which their families differ. On the board, list the categories horizontally along the bottom. On the vertical axis, list the number of children from zero to the total number in the class. Then as you count the families represented in each category, mark the total on the chart and fill in the bars. Possible categories include:
- One parent
- Two parents

- Grandparent
- Other adult
- Children under 5
- Children 5 to 12
- Children 13 to 21
- African American
- Asian
- Hispanic
- White
- Pets

Discussion Questions

1. Why do we live in families?
2. How do we benefit by living in families?
3. What new information did you learn about a classmate by looking at his or her family portrait?
4. Which family portraits contain something that makes you curious to know more?

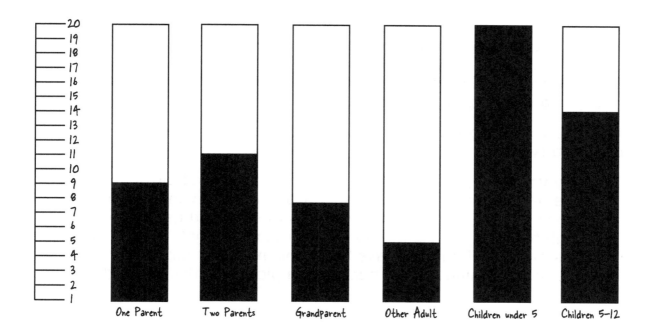

Thoughtful Gifts

The children invent endings to a story about gift-giving and draw pictures illustrating their conclusions. Through experiences such as these, the children learn the value of caring and thoughtful behaviors

Objectives

The children will:
- practice good listening.
- create a logical ending to a simple story.
- identify thoughtful behaviors and special favors that make good "gifts."

Materials

drawing materials

Procedure

Tell the children that you want them to listen very carefully while you read them the beginning of a story. Explain that the story has no ending, and that the job of each student will be to create an ending for the story and draw a picture of that ending.

Distribute the drawing materials before reading one or both of the following story-starters.

1. A very young boy wants to give his mother a special birthday gift, but he has no money—not a dollar, or a dime, or even a penny. This boy doesn't know anyone who has money, and he isn't old enough to get a job. He is very worried that he won't have a gift for his mother. Then, two days before his mother's birthday, he thinks of something to give her. Draw a picture of the boy and his gift.

2. Two weeks before Christmas, your parents tell you that they don't want you to buy a gift for them. Instead, they want you to do something special for them—something that will please them and make them happy. Draw a picture of yourself doing something for your parents at Christmas.

Have the children take turns showing and explaining their conclusion to the story. Use this sharing process to stimulate discussion about the importance of intention, thoughtfulness, and sentiment in gift-giving.

Discussion Questions

1. What were some of the gifts that people gave in their stories?
2. What are some other gifts that don't cost any money?
3. What is something you can do to make your mother happy without spending a dime? What about your father? What could you do for your teacher?
4. How difficult was it to think of something to draw?
5. What could someone do for you instead of buying you a gift?

Learning About Family Backgrounds

In this activity the children learn to
recognize and respect the differences in
various family backgrounds while they share
information about their own heritage gained
from interviews with their parents and/or
grandparents.

Objectives

The children will:
- learn facts about their family
  background and the backgrounds of classmates.
- identify countries and cities of origin and learn something about
  them.
- gain an understanding of the diversity represented within the
  class.

Materials

world, U.S., and regional maps

Procedure

Have the children ask their parents and/or grandparents where
they were born. Ask them to find out how and why their parents or
grandparents came to the U.S. from another country, or to your part
of the country from another region.

Give the children a list of questions to ask their parents/grandparents,
including:
- What was your purpose in moving?
- What was it like to leave your home and go where you didn't
  know anyone and had no idea what to expect?
- What things were the same in both countries/regions, and what
  things were different?

- What are some problems people encounter when they move to a new place?
- How long did it take you to make friends in your new home?

Post the maps where everyone can see them. As the children take turns sharing the information obtained from their families, use flags or other markers to indicate the places on the map where parents/grandparents lived. Help the children gain an understanding of the distances traveled. Talk about the modes of transportation used and emphasize the differences between travel today and travel in earlier times.

Create a chart showing how many countries and states of origin are represented in the class. Include a place on the chart for native children. Make sure that the names of all of the children are included.

Discussion Questions

1. What is the most interesting thing you learned from your parents/grandparents that you never knew before?
2. How do you stay in touch with relatives who live far away?
3. Why is it important to learn about the places our families came from?
4. How can we benefit as a class by having people from many different backgrounds?

Who Works in Our Neighborhood?

The children study the composition of the neighborhood surrounding their after-school site and create a mural showing representative businesses, homes, and other features. Through this activity, the children develop an understanding of how people collaborate to build functioning communities that serve everyone.

Objectives

The children will:
- identify individuals and businesses that reside in the neighborhood surrounding their after-school site.
- describe roles played by the employees of neighborhood stores and businesses.

Materials

a long roll of plain white paper, such as shelf paper; colored marking pens; masking tape

Procedure

Initiate a class discussion by asking the children, "Who lives and works in the neighborhood around our after-school?" As the children recall people, list names and job titles or descriptions on the board or chart paper. Encourage the children to think of different store employees (supermarket, drug store, post office, etc.) along with firefighters, police officers, friends, and neighbors. If the children fail to include the after-school and its employees, remind them that these buildings and the people in them are part of the neighborhood, too. If possible, take a walk around the neighborhood. Point out buildings, stores, and streets, and ask questions such as, "Who lives there?" and "Who works in that store?"

If computers are available, appoint children to conduct an Internet search to find the web sites of some of the neighborhood businesses. Ask them to report their findings to the class, adding to the information already obtained.

Attach a long sheet of paper to one wall. Distribute the art materials. Have the children make a mural of the neighborhood. Help them decide who will be responsible for each part of the mural. Make sure that all of the children have a role in the mural's creation. Continue discussion of the neighborhood and its people as the children work. Help everyone understand that the people who live and work in the area are important, and that they share responsibility for creating a cooperative neighborhood.

Discussion Questions
1. Where could you go for help if you got into some kind of trouble while walking home from after-school?
2. How do some of the nearby stores contribute to our after-school?
3. What is the most interesting thing you learned about a nearby business?
4. Which neighborhood stores have you or your parents shopped in or visited? What did you buy or do there?

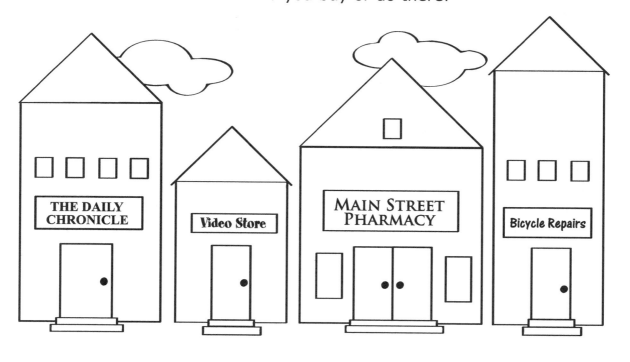

Who Works Here?

In this activity the children learn about the various roles people play in making their after-school function and come to understand the importance of dependability in any job function.

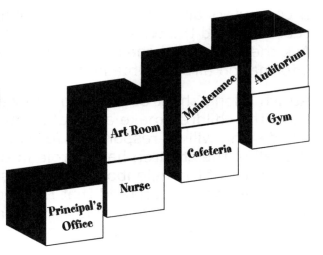

Objectives

The children will:
- identify jobs performed at their after school (or school).
- gain awareness of specific tasks necessary to make an after-school run smoothly.
- simulate interactions between after-school employees through role play.

Materials

building blocks or other easily movable objects

Procedure

Ask the children to name jobs held at your after-school. If the after-school is located at the regular school, have the children name the school and after-school jobs performed throughout the day. Help them to name as many positions as possible, including teachers, aides, principal, secretaries, custodians, social workers, counselors, bus drivers, and cafeteria workers. Compile a list on the board.

Take a tour of the school or after-school site to see the employees doing their work. Check with several individuals ahead of time and identify four or five who are willing to describe and demonstrate what they do in their jobs.

When you return to the room, discuss the different tasks that the children observed being performed. Help the children to understand that everyone in the after-school has an important function and that, in order for it to run smoothly, all workers must cooperate and contribute to its success.

Have the children work together to make a big floor plan of the after-school using building blocks or easily movable objects. The plan doesn't need to be an accurate replica, merely representative of all the places visited by the children when they took their tour. Encourage the children to act out the different roles they observed, using the floor plan as a prop.

Discussion Questions

1. Which jobs did you learn about for the first time?
2. Which job interests you the most?
3. What are some of the duties of the people who work in the office?
4. Who repairs playground equipment when it breaks?
5. Who decides what the lunch menu will be each day?
6. What would happen if someone didn't show up to do their job? (the bus driver, the cafeteria worker, your teacher, etc.)
7. How does it help you when you can count on others to do their jobs?

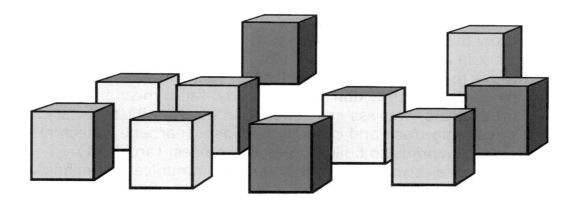

Identifying Careers

Objectives

The children will:
- identify occupations based on clues in a game.
- describe jobs that are present in the child's community and beyond.

Materials

large game boards or copies of the game board provided (enough for every pair of competing teams); buttons or other markers, index cards on which to write the occupational clues listed below

Procedure

Prepare in advance the index cards by printing the occupational "clues" listed below with one clue on each card. Prepare enough sets of cards so that each pair of competing teams has a complete set. Do not include the answers written in parentheses.

- I write stories for you and your parents to read. (author)
- I build houses for you to live in. (construction worker)
- I help keep places from being robbed (security guard)
- I raise cattle and pigs so you have meat to eat. (rancher)
- I change the colors of rooms and houses to those you like. (painter)
- I practice many hours so you can enjoy the music I play. (musician)
- I go to the factory to build cars. (factory worker)
- I grow the crops you eat like corn, tomatoes and carrots. (farmer)
- I work in a store and sell you clothing. (sales clerk)
- I move to music and wear costumes. (dancer)
- I fix cars when they don't run properly. (auto mechanic)
- I type letters, address envelopes, and open mail. (secretary)
- I drive a big truck and collect your trash. (garbage collector)
- I draw blueprints to build homes and offices. (architect)
- I hook up electronics in your house. (communication technician)
- I tell you the news on television every night. (newscaster)
- I take your food order in the restaurant. (server/wait person)
- I bake bread and sweet rolls for you to eat. (baker)
- I help people when they are sick. (doctor/nurse)
- I help children learn to read and write. (teacher)
- I deliver packages and letters to your house. (mailman)

- I work in a store and sell you rings and watches. (jeweler)
- I clean your teeth and fill your cavities. (dentist)
- I put the pipes in your house so the water will run and I unclog your drains when there is a problem. (plumber)
- I write songs for you to enjoy. (composer/songwriter)
- I drive a truck and put out the fires. (firefighter)
- I paint and draw beautiful pictures. (artist)
- I fly the plane to take you to new and wonderful places. (pilot)
- I serve you food and drinks on a plane. (flight attendant)
- I work with computers and design programs. (programmer)
- I design bridges, tunnels, and freeways. (engineer)

Introduce the activity by explaining to the children that they will be playing a board game where they will be competing to identify careers. Divide the children into teams of four or five. After the teams have been selected, identify the competing teams and have the teams spread out around the room so they can play without hearing the answers from other teams.

Give each team a button or marker and a deck of clue cards (face down). Have the teams flip a coin to decide who will go first. Explain that they must try to correctly name occupations based on the clues they draw from the deck of cards. The first player on TEAM A draws a card, reads the clue aloud, and names the occupation. If he or she answers correctly, TEAM A moves its game-board marker ahead one square. Then a second player on TEAM A draws a card and repeats the process. When a TEAM A player answers incorrectly TEAM B takes over the play. The team that finishes first wins.

Note:

If your students are very adept, you may wish to impose an arbitrary limit to the number of consecutive plays that a given team may have before turning over play to the other team. For example, tell the students that after three correct answers (and moves on the game board), play automatically reverts to the opposing team.

Discussion Questions
1. Do you know anyone who works in one of the careers in the game?
2. Is there any career named that you might like to be in someday?
3. What kinds of things would you like to do when you grow up?

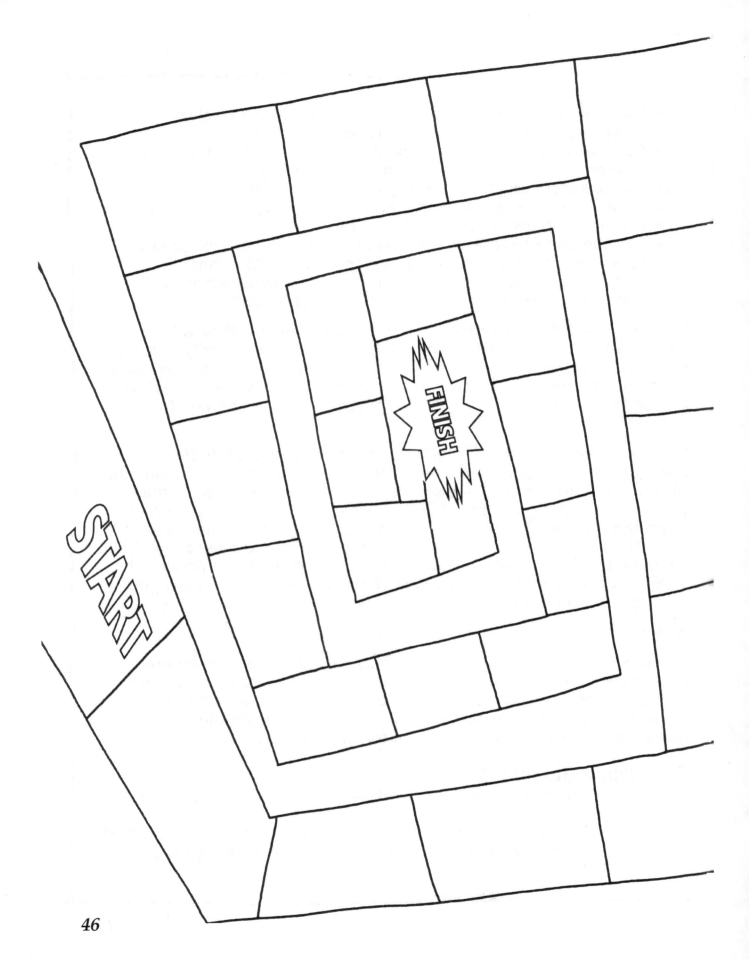

Communicating with Others

Creating and Sharing Greeting Cards

In this activity the children learn about the importance of friendly greetings by viewing and discussing different types of greeting cards and the messages they include. They then make and deliver greeting cards to people they know. In an extension activity, they create cards for children in another class or pediatric patients in a hospital.

Objectives

The children will:
- distinguish between different categories of greeting cards.
- identify words and phrases in greeting cards that have meaning for them.
- create and deliver greeting cards to people of their choosing.
- compose appropriate messages for the types of cards they create.

Materials

a variety of greeting cards that you, or someone in your family, have received; pre-cut half-sheets of sturdy paper (5 ½ × 8 ½); colored marking pens or crayons, decorative items such as stars, lace, sequins, and glitter; glue; the list of favorite words and phrases (developed during the activity) posted where everyone can see it

Procedure

Begin this activity by asking the children to tell how they feel when they receive a birthday card, get-well card, valentine card, or holiday card. Ask, "How do you think other people feel when they receive a card from you?"

Tell the children that you would like to share with them some of the cards that you (or someone in your family) have received from others. On a bulletin board or very large sheet of butcher paper, label a column for each type of card (Get-well, Birthday, Valentine, Friendship, Easter, Christmas, Hanukkah, etc.).

Read each card and ask the children to decide in which column the card belongs. Tape the card in the correct column. Then, have the children name words or phrases from both outside and inside the cards that they like and might include in a greeting card that they make and send to someone. List the words on the board or chart paper.

If you have easy access to computers, suggest that the children research greeting card sites on the Internet. Give them opportunities to browse selections in pairs and choose their favorite cards to show the class.

Next, ask the children to think of a special person (family member, friend, neighbor) whom they would like to surprise with a greeting card.

Distribute the paper and art materials. Direct the children to fold their paper in half so that it is the size and shape of a greeting card, and to create a design or picture on the front that symbolizes the type of card they intend to send. To generate ideas, ask them to name things that would be appropriate for a birthday card (cake, presents, balloons, candles), a get-well card (flowers, smiley face, pets), and other types of cards. Suggest that those who wish may glue decorative items to their cards.

Have each child write a message on the inside of his or her card. Assist younger children to write or dictate a message for the inside of the card. Point to the list of favorite words and phrases that the children chose and remind them that they may copy from the list. When the cards are finished, have each child share his or her card with the rest of the group. Urge the children to hand deliver their greeting cards as soon as possible. A few days later, spend some time talking about the experience and the reactions the cards generated.

Discussion Questions

1. Why do people like to send greeting cards to one another?
2. When was the last time you sent a greeting card to someone? Was it a regular card or an electronic card?
3. What does the word greeting mean?
4. What other kinds of greetings do we use to communicate with others?

In an extension activity (or as an alternative), write the names of children from a neighboring class on paper strips and put them in a box or bag. Have each child draw a name and create a friendship greeting card for that child. Or have the children create encouraging cards for pediatric patients at a local hospital. Place all of the cards in a large envelope and address it to the hospital. Include a cover letter, which the children dictate to you. Deliver or mail the cards, as appropriate.

Discussion Questions for the Extension Activity

1. Do you know how the person who received your card reacted? How?
2. How do you think the person felt?
3. How did you feel after making and delivering the card?
4. What did you learn about the messages inside greeting cards?

Sounds Around!

This is both a listening and writing activity in which the children use attentive listening to differentiate and identify sounds in the environment. They try to replicate the sounds with their voices and with instruments. Finally, they label the sounds and use the labels to create a story.

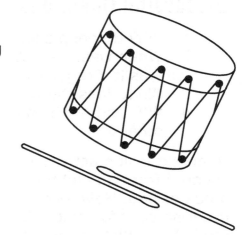

Objectives

The children will:
- practice attentive listening.
- identify and describe environmental sounds.
- replicate sounds using vocal tones and rhythmic instruments.
- create a story based on "sound words."

Materials

rhythm instruments

Procedure

Have the children sit quietly and listen to all of the sounds around them. After several minutes of quiet listening, ask the children to name, or briefly describe, the sounds they heard while you list them on the board. For example:

shuffling of feet
ticking of clock
banging of door
sound of a car starting (ignition)

Take the children outdoors and repeat the procedure, listing the sounds on a note pad.

Back in the room, ask the children to reproduce the sounds they heard—first with their voices and then with rhythmic instruments. Ask them if they can think of words to describe the sounds they are making (loud, soft, clicking, humming, etc.). List these "sound words" separately. When you have a lengthy list, use the words to write a group story. For example:

Andy was humming a tune on his way to school. The soft clicking of the bicycle spokes kept time. He stopped singing and swerved when a loud car passed him going way too fast. Etc.

An alternative method of creating a story is to go around the class and ask each child to contribute one word. To elicit more words, go around several times. Use a recording device to record the story, or simply write it down as it develops. Play (or read) back the completed story and discuss the results. Help the children to understand that in order to add a word that makes sense, they must listen to the words that came before.

Discussion Questions

1. What gives meaning to a sentence?
2. How can our story be improved?
3. What sounds did you hear today that you usually ignore? Why do you think you don't always hear those sounds?
4. What is your favorite sound?
5. What did you learn today by listening very carefully?
6. What is the difference between hearing something and really listening to something?

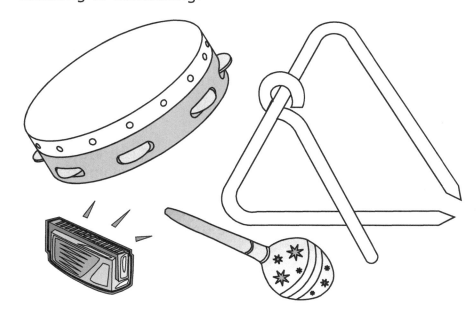

Communicating Clearly

This activity gives children an opportunity to learn and to practice good communication skills.

Objectives

The children will:
- practice simple rules of good communication.
- recognize that poor communication results in misunderstandings.

Materials

Procedure

Begin by talking with the children about how much we depend on our ability to communicate with one another. Mention that communication is one of those things that can be very good or very bad. Bad communication leads to misunderstandings. It can cause people to get directions wrong, make mistakes, and feel hurt or angry.

On the board, write the following guidelines of good communication. Go over them and talk about why each is important if people want to get along and understand each other.

1. Look at the other person.
2. Listen carefully.
3. Speak clearly.
4. Think about what you want to say.
5. Say what you mean.

Have the children form groups of three to five. Describe one of the situations on the next page to each group, and explain that you want them to act it out using good communication. Give the groups 10 to 15 minutes to plan and rehearse their skits. Then have one group at a time perform its skit for the entire group. Circulate and provide assistance during the planning period by helping the children identify and understand the good communication skills they can demonstrate in their skits. Use these and your own questions to facilitate discussion after each skit is performed.

Discussion Questions

1. Did the actors look at each other while they were communicating?
2. How well did they listen?
3. Could they have expressed themselves more clearly? How?
4. What else could they have said?
5. What happened as a result of this communication?
6. What have you learned about good communication?

Situations

- You are looking for a missing book and think that a group of children might have it or know where it is.
- Someone asks to play on your team, but you already have enough kids.
- You and your friends must decide what each person will bring to a picnic.
- You don't understand what the teacher has asked you to do.
- You want to meet and make friends with a new student.
- You want to eat lunch with kids you usually don't eat with.
- All the kids around you are whispering and making noise, so you can't hear what the teacher is saying.

Creative Sound

A game format is used to have children guess the sources of many different sounds. Then they create items that make distinctive sounds. This encourage both attentive listening and creative thinking.

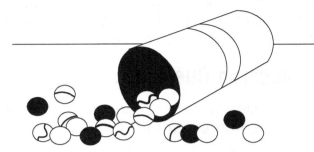

Objectives

The children will:
- identify the sources of a variety of sounds.
- find or make items that make distinctive sounds.
- describe the sounds that they make and hear.

Materials

a large box filled with items, each of which makes a unique sound. Examples are marbles in a can, beans in a small box, sound blocks, a pie tin, a whistle, a clock, a pair of wooden spoons.

Procedure

Have all of the children close their eyes and put their heads down on their desks or tables. Ask one child at a time to select an item from the box and create a sound with it. Without looking, have the rest of the class try to guess the identity of the item. If the class is unable to guess correctly, allow the performing child to offer descriptive clues, such as, "You might use these to mix a cake," or "Small, round, and colorful."

If the children still cannot guess, have the performer return the item to the box so that the children can open their eyes. Then encourage the children to discuss what the noise sounded like, giving examples and using descriptive words.

Have the child who correctly identifies the item become the next performer.

Next, tell the children that they are going to create their own "Sound Machine." Ask them to use their creativity and find or make something that produces a distinctive sound. Tell them they can use items from the room or from outdoors. Allow time for the children to "create" their sound machines. Circulate and help as needed.

When all the children have completed the task, have one child at a time beat out a rhythm using his or her "sound machine." Then have the other children attempt to produce the same rhythm with their own sound machines.

After the children have had an opportunity to mimic several different rhythm patterns, ask them to beat out the rhythm of familiar songs. Have the children form small groups and perform songs for the rest of the group. Encourage the children to be creative and inventive with their "Sound Machines" and performances.

Discussion Questions

1. What was your favorite sound today?
2. How did you come up with the item for you "Sound Machine"?
3. What sound have you heard today that sounds like something else?
4. How do you think sound effects are made in movies and TV shows?
5. How is making sounds for others to hear and listening carefully to the sounds you hear like what happens in a conversation?

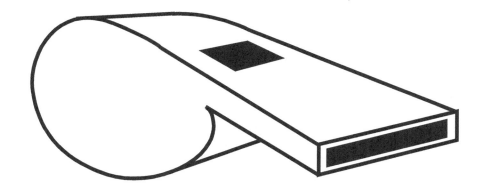

The Sound of Numbers

In this activity the children develop auditory discrimination skills through trial and error in a game with marbles. For younger children this also becomes a lesson in counting as they choose and guess the number of marbles used.

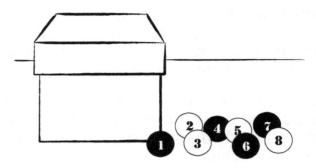

Objectives

The children will:
- compare the sounds produced by the interaction of different numbers of marbles.
- attempt to correctly identify the correct number of marbles using auditory clues in repeated trials.

Materials

marbles (eight times the number of children in the class, plus extras), a small box for each child

Procedure

Begin the activity with a demonstration using eight marbles and a box. Gather the children around so that everyone can see. Place all eight marbles in the box, cover it, and shake the box for several seconds. Direct the children to listen to the sound that is produced.

Next, have the children close their eyes while you remove several marbles from the box. Cover and shake the box again. Ask the children, "Are there more or fewer marbles in the box?" See if the children can guess the number of marbles remaining in the box. Open the box and count them together. Continue the demonstration for several minutes, varying the number of marbles in the box.

Give a box and eight marbles to each child. Have the children pair up. Ask them to decide who is "A" and who is "B" (or some other designation).

Walk the pairs through the steps of a similar game. While the A's close their eyes, have the B's put some marbles in their boxes and shake them. Have the A's listen and then attempt to replicate the sounds by putting the same number in their boxes.

The A's can then add or subtract marbles until the sounds their boxes produce are the same as the sounds coming from B's boxes. The partners then open their boxes and compare numbers.

Have the children switch roles and play the game at least once more. As time allows, let them continue to play.

Discussion Questions

1. How is the sound of eight marbles different from the sound of three?
2. How difficult was it to guess the correct numbers?
3. Was guessing correctly easier at the low end or the high end?
4. When we want to listen for something very carefully, we often close our eyes. Why do we do that?
5. When you are having a conversation with someone, why is it important to listen carefully to what the other person is saying?
6. How does it make you feel when someone listens to you?

Junk Art

Objectives

The children will:
- demonstrate positive skills for interacting with and relating to others.
- describe the importance of cooperation when working with others.

Materials

a large collection of varied kinds of "junk," such as paper towel tubes, scraps of materials, bits of scrap wood, buttons, beads, sequins, bits of colored yarn, string, nails, screws, and other things in different shapes and sizes to be used to create an art montage; kraft paper and glue

Procedure

Introduce the activity by telling the children that they are going to be using odds and ends, or junk, to make interesting creations. Divide the children into pairs. Ask the partners to work as a team to select several pieces of junk and then to glue their junk to a piece of kraft paper to create a relief design. Explain that the object can look like something real, such as a car or horse, or it can be an abstract design, but that each pair must work together to decide on the design and then to create it.

Allow time for the children to work together, circulate and offer help and comment on how well they are working together. When the children finish their design work have them share their creations with the entire group.

Use the following questions along with those of your own to encourage the children to talk about the experience of communicating and working cooperatively as a team.

Discussion Questions

1. In what ways was it fun to make something from junk?
2. How did you and your partner decide what your design should be?
3. What kinds of problems did you have working with a partner?
4. Why is it important that people help each other when they work together?
5. Why is communicating important when you work as a team?

Cooperating with Others

Giving Clear Directions

The familiar "pin-the-tail" game requires precise communication. In this activity the children play in pairs to add the elements of cooperation and trust.

Objectives

The children will:
- practice giving and receiving precise verbal instructions.
- appreciate the importance of clear, accurate communication.
- work cooperatively with a partner.

Materials

blindfold, pins, either a pin-the-tail on the donkey game that you bring in or use the template provided of pin-the-ball on the seal's nose game

Procedure

Talk with the children about the importance of communicating clearly and accurately. Tell them that they are going to practice giving clear directions and listening carefully by playing the familiar game, "Pin the Tail on the Donkey" (or "Pin the Ball on the Seal's Nose").

Post the target of the donkey (or seal) in an area clear of desks, chairs, and other obstacles.

Ask the children to form pairs. Explain that the partners must work together in order to win the game. One partner must give very clear, accurate instructions, and the other must follow them very carefully to try to pin the tail on the donkey (or the ball on the seal's nose).

Have the first pair come forward. Blindfold one child and spin him or her around a few feet from the target. Then step aside and have the child's partner guide the child to the target using only words. Make certain that the tail (or ball) is pinned securely to the donkey (or seal) before removing the blindfold. Repeat the procedure with the remaining pairs. Award a prize to the pair whose tail (or ball) is closest to the correct spot on the target. Have the partners switch roles and play the game again.

Conclude the activity with a discussion.

Discussion Questions

1. What was hard about giving directions?
2. What was difficult about following directions?
3. When you were blindfolded, how confident were you that your partner would not let you get into trouble?
4. Why is it so important to communicate clearly in this game? ...to listen carefully?
5. What are some examples of other situations in which it would be important to communicate very clearly and to listen carefully?

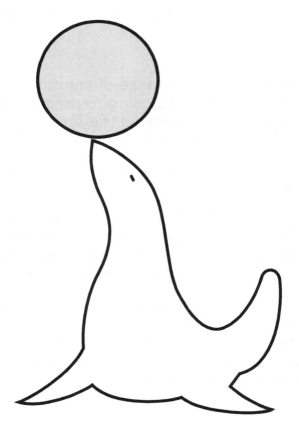

Making and Keeping Friends

It's important for children to feel like they are accepted by others and have friends they can count on. In this activity the children learn friendship skills and act out real-life situations that can help them to make friends and to be a good friend to others.

Objectives:

The children will:
- describe behaviors that facilitate friendships
- demonstrate desirable skills for interacting with and relating to others
- demonstrate tolerance and flexibility in group situations

Procedure:

Lead a discussion on friendship by saying in your own words to the children:

"We all want to be treated in friendly ways. One of the best ways to be treated well ourselves is to be a good friend to others and treat them well. So let's talk about friendship today. Let's act out, and show one another, how friendship really works. To get started, let's make a list of some ways to make friends- ways that work well. Then we'll make a list of ways to keep a friend.

Write the heading, "Making Friends" on the board and list the strategies that the children describe. Do the same under the heading "Keeping Friends". Add any additional strategies that you think are important.

Next, tell the children that you have some ideas for situations they can act out using the strategies on the list. Have the children form groups of three or four. Assign one of the situations listed on the next page to each group and tell them to plan and perform a role-play of that situation. Give half the groups a situation from the "Making Friends" list and the other half from the "Keeping Friends" list.

Give the groups time to plan and rehearse their role-plays. Circulate and observe the rehearsals. Assist with planning as necessary. Make sure all the children have a role to play when they act out their situations.

When the children have finished rehearsing, have each group take a turn acting out its situation. Use the Discussions Question to facilitate a discussion after each performance.

Discussion Questions:

1. Why is it helpful for us to think of something that we do to keep friends? To make friends?
2. What are some behaviors that cause people to loose friends?
3. What have you learned that can help you keep friends? ...make a friend?

Situations for the "Making Friends" Role-Plays

1. You are playing a game with some of your friends in your front yard. A new girl in the neighborhood walks up and stands nearby watching.

2. The teacher asks you and a boy in your class whom you don't know very well to take a box of books to the library. You believe this boy is much smarter than you are.

3. A family of a different race moves into a house on your street. The family includes two children about your age. One day the children come out of the house just as you walk by on your way to school.

Situations for the "Keeping Friends" Role-Plays

1. Your friend calls you, but you just sat down to dinner with your family and it isn't a good time to talk.

2. Your friend had a fight with her big sister and is feeling terrible.

3. You are at the movies with a friend. Just before it starts, another friend comes over and sits beside you and says, "Hi." These two friends of yours don't know each other.

Mirror My Pose

In this cooperative activity the children assume poses in response to specific words. They work in pairs, with one partner mirroring the poses of the other. This experience helps children understand that we can convey information and feelings through our "body language".

Objectives:

The children will:
- assume the role of leader in a simple game.
- practice the role of follower.
- demonstrate their understanding of vocabulary words through physical responses.

Materials

Procedure

Have the children get together in pairs. Tell them to decide who is "A" and who is "B." Explain that you will read a word to the class, and the A's will strike a pose showing the meaning of the word, or what they think of in response to the word. Explain that there are no right or wrong responses, so whatever they come up with is okay. However, it must be a still pose, not a series of movements. For example, if the word is "scary," they might pose like a scary monster. Tell them to hold the pose until you tell them it's okay to move again.

Explain that the B's are to face their partners and mirror the pose, mimicking as many details as possible. They, too, must hold the pose until you tell them to move. Then they will switch roles. When you read the next word, the B's will strike a pose and the A's will mimic it.

Choose words from the list below, or select others that you think will be fun and challenging.

- happy
- a bunny
- sad
- brave
- a pretzel
- a bird
- soggy
- hot
- crisp
- cold
- excited
- friendly
- curious
- polite
- sleepy
- angry
- a kitten

After the first four or five rounds, have the children change partners. Continue the process. Conclude the activity with a discussion.

Discussion Questions

1. Which word did you most enjoy portraying?
2. Which role was more difficult, inventing a pose or mirroring a pose?
3. When you mirror someone, how is your pose different from theirs?
4. Which was the most difficult word to portray?
5. What did you learn about how we can communicate feelings without using words?

Peanut Butter Sculptures

In this cooperative, decision-making activity the children work in pairs to create a joint sculpture out of "peanut play dough." In an extension, they use peanut butter to mortar crackers into sculptures of varying shapes.

Objectives

The children will:
- cooperate to create a sculpture.
- use problem-solving skills to plan their approach to a task.

Materials

for the lead activity: peanut butter, dry milk, honey, plastic knives and spoons to use as sculpting tools (optional)

for the extension: peanut butter, crackers in different shapes

Procedure

Prepare the "play dough." For a new twist on play dough, use the following recipe:

    1/2 cup peanut butter
    1/2 cup nonfat dry milk
    2/3 tablespoon honey

Mix the peanut butter and dry milk. Add the honey. Mix and knead until you achieve a good dough-like consistency. Refrigerate in a covered container. Peanut play dough can be eaten, modeled, stretched, pounded and rolled; however, it does not harden well. Do not plan to have the children keep their creations for long.

Have the children form pairs. Give some dough to each pair. Have them use the dough to create a sculpture. Instruct them to talk it over and decide on a subject for their sculpture, and then to take turns working on it, or work on it simultaneously. Urge them to share the work equally.

Have each pair show their finished sculpture to the class. Ask them to explain what their sculpture represents and how they came to that decision. After everyone has shared, allow the children to eat their sculptures.

Extension

Distribute crackers and peanut butter. Working in pairs, have the children build sculptures by putting together interesting configurations using the peanut butter as mortar to hold the crackers together. After sharing, allow the children to eat their sculptures.

NOTE: If the children are going to eat their creations, make sure that they wash their hands before beginning to work with the dough.

Discussion Questions

1. How did you decide on a subject for your sculpture?
2. How did you work together, by taking turns or in some other way?
3. Did you work on different parts of the sculpture, or did you both work on every part of the sculpture?
4. How did you handle any disagreements you had?

Chair Volleyball

In this lively activity the children learn teamwork behaviors as they cooperate with a partner in a volleyball-like game in which they play on their knees against other pairs.

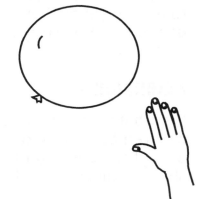

Objectives

The children will:
- work with a partner to achieve a simple objective.
- practice cooperation and teamwork.

Materials

round balloons (one for each pair of children, plus extras), moveable chairs

Procedure

Ask the children to form pairs. Have the pairs spread out around the room. Make sure that each pair has a chair and plenty of space in which to move around. Distribute the balloons. Help the children blow up and tie their balloons.

Ask for a show of hands from the children who have played volleyball. Explain that they are going to play volleyball in pairs, using their balloons as balls and the backs of their chairs as nets. One person will be on one side of the chair, and the other person will be on the opposite side. However, they will not be playing against each other. Each pair is a team and must cooperate to keep their ball in the air as long as possible. All of the pairs will play at once and the pair whose balloon stays in the air longest will win.

Announce one last rule: The children must play on their knees.

Have the children get down on their knees on opposite sides of their chairs, with one child ready to "serve" the balloon. Signal the start of the game. Watch all the pairs. When a pair drops or breaks their balloon, call them out of the game. Allow the game to continue until only one pair remains. Proclaim that pair the winners. Have the children change partners, and continue with additional rounds.

Discussion Questions

1. What did you have to do to keep your balloon in the air?
2. What was it like to play on your knees?
3. Where did you keep your eyes, on the balloon, your partner, or somewhere else?
4. What kinds of movements helped and what kinds made things worse?
5. What did you partner do that was helpful? ...not helpful?
6. How did you and your partner demonstrate cooperation?

Group Break In

In this fun and lively cooperative game the children are learning about what it feels like to be excluded and, ultimately through discussion, considering the value in making room for everyone.

Objectives

The children will:
- describe the importance of cooperation to accomplishing a task
- describe what it is like to be excluded from a group
- identify and describe ways of being included in a group

Materials

Procedure

Locate a large, open space where the children can move about freely and make noise.

Number the children off randomly to form groups of seven or eight. Say to them that they will be given a task to perform as a group. One person will stand outside each group and try to break in, while the other children form a tight circle with their arms locked together to keep the person out. The person outside the circle must try his or her best to get inside the circle and the group must try equally hard to keep that person out.

Tell the children that they are not to make it easier for friends. Everyone is given 2 minutes to try whatever they think will work (talking, climbing, etc.) to get into the circle and every child will have a turn to be on the outside.

When a child succeeds in getting into the circle or when time runs out

Cooperating with Others

that person becomes a part of the circle and another child will take his or her turn on the outside.

Expect lots of laughter and shouting. Be prepared for frustration on the part of the person trying to break in. Continue the game until all the children have had an opportunity to be on the outside.

When the game concludes, gather the groups together and ask them to talk about their experiences by using the following questions or those of your own.

Discussion Questions

1. What did it feel like to be outside the group?
2. What did it feel like to be part of the group?
3. Did your group cooperate? What was your common purpose?
4. As a group member, was it more difficult to keep a friend out than someone you didn't know quite so well?
5. How did it feel to succeed a getting in? ...to fail?
6. What were some of the ways you used to keep others out of the circle?
7. What do we do to keep others out of our activities in real life?
8. How has this experience changed your feelings about being included and excluded?
9. What are some things you can do to help others be included in your activities?

Friendly Flowers

In this craft project, the children talk about what friendliness and understanding mean to them, and then they create baskets of paper flowers, with each flower representing a friendly or understanding quality.

Objectives

The children will:
- define the words friendly and understanding.
- identify qualities and characteristics of friendly and understanding people.
- complete a craft project symbolizing friendliness and understanding.

Materials

colored construction paper for making flowers; green construction paper for making stems and leaves of different sizes; brown construction paper for making baskets;pencils, scissors, glue, and marking pens

Procedure

Write the heading "friendly" on the board. Ask the children what the word means. Talk about its definition. Ask the children to think of words that describe and encourage friendliness between people. List the words that they suggest on the board. For example:

- sharing
- smiling
- warm
- caring

- outgoing
- agreeable
- easygoing
- happy

Next, write the heading "understanding" on the board. Follow the same procedure, listing characteristics such as:

- kind
- thoughtful
- forgiving

- considerate
- patient
- giving

Tell the children that they are going to create baskets filled with paper flowers that represent some of the characteristics of friendly and understanding people.

Distribute the colored construction paper, marking pens, scissors and glue. Have the children draw flower shapes on the colored paper and then cut out the lowers. Help your children as necessary with the shapes and cutting. Next, instruct the children to choose one word from either list and write it in the center of a flower. Tell them to write a different word on each flower.

Distribute the green construction paper, pencils, and scissors. Show the children how to draw stems and leaves of different sizes, cut them out, and glue them to the flowers. Circulate and assist as the children work.

Distribute the brown construction paper and show the children how to cut out a basket shape. Show the children how to glue their flowers to the back of the basket. Circulate and assist them to complete their baskets of flowers. Display the flowers on tables and desks around the room.

Use these and your own questions to stimulate discussion about friendly and understanding behavior

Discussion Questions

1. How do you know when someone is friendly?
2. How can you tell when a person is understanding?
3. Is it possible to be friendly with everyone?
4. When is it important to be understanding?

The Reason for Rules

A good way to help children develop an understanding of rules and the necessity for having them is to involve them in a discussion. In this activity, the children discuss the meaning and purpose of various rules. Afterwards, they create posters depicting chosen rules.

Objectives

The children will:
- name school, after-school, home, and community rules.
- understand and explain the purpose of rules.

Materials

construction paper or poster board; colored marking pens, paints, or crayons

Procedure

Begin by asking the children to think of rules they are expected to obey at school, at after-school, at home, and in the community. Call on volunteers to state various rules while you write them on the board. Examples of possible rules are:

School
- Do not leave class without permission.
- No talking during tests.
- Listen to the teacher.
- No cutting in line.

After-school
- Don't leave until an authorized adult comes to pick you up.
- No running in the halls
- No hitting or pushing.
- Share toys and books.

No Running in the Halls

Home

- No TV or video games until homework is done.
- Pick up and put away toys you are not using.
- Don't leave the property without parent permission.
- Do your chores without being told.

Community

- No skateboarding on city sidewalks and streets.
- Cross streets at corners and within crosswalks.
- Obey traffic signals.
- No littering.

When you have a lengthy list of rules, take a look at each one. Ask the children:

- Why do we have this rule?
- Who or what is the rule designed to protect?
- What would happen if we didn't have this rule?
- Is this a necessary rule, or an unnecessary rule?

Facilitate discussion, encouraging the children to actually think about the rules instead of merely accepting and obeying, or resenting and ignoring, them without question.

As a follow-up to the discussion, have the children each choose a rule that they consider important and create a poster depicting that rule. Suggest that they print the rule in large letters and draw a picture of a child or adult obeying or disobeying the rule. When finished, allow each child to hold up his or her poster and tell the group why they chose that role. Display the posters around the room.

Discussion Questions

1. Who makes the rules in your home? ...at our school? ...in our after-school class?
2. Who makes the rules in our city?
3. What would our after-school group be like if we all did exactly as we pleased?
4. If you could make a new rule for school or home, what would it be?

Who Will Win the Race?

After listening to a version of the classic story about the tortoise and the hare, the children discuss the story's lessons regarding speed and carelessness versus steadfastness and determination.

Objectives

The children will:
- discuss possible advantages of persistence and speed.
- name instances when speed is appropriate and inappropriate.

Materials

art and/or writing materials

Procedure

Read aloud the story, "Slow and Steady Wins the Race." After the story, facilitate a class discussion about the story's meaning and lessons.

As a follow-up to the story, have the children draw a picture of one part of the story and/or write their own version of the story.

Discussion Questions

1. What was more important in this race, being fast or being tireless and determined?
2. What was Mr. Rabbit's mistake?
3. Would you say that Mr. Rabbit was careless? Why?
4. Have you ever lost something or made a mistake because you were careless? When?
5. When is it necessary to hurry?
6. Name a time when it is not safe or necessary to hurry.
7. Is it better to do a big assignment a little at a time and very carefully, or all at once and in a hurry? Why?

Slow and Steady Wins the Race

Once upon a time there lived a big gray rabbit with little red eyes who always bragged that he could run faster than any animal in the forest. After weeks and months of bragging, he had made all the other animals angry. They were tired of hearing him brag about how fast he was.

One morning, old Mr. Turtle, who was always slow but very thoughtful and would never ever brag about anything, said to Mr. Rabbit, "Why do you have to brag about yourself so much? Certainly you are fast. All the animals can see that. But even you can be beaten."

"Hah, hah," laughed Mr. Rabbit. "Me, get beaten? Ha, hah, hah. And just who do think can beat me? Certainly not you," he challenged.

At that, old Mr. Turtle looked the big gray rabbit right in the eye and said, "I accept your challenge and will race you tomorrow morning. But you just may be surprised by who wins."

News of the race spread quickly. That afternoon, the forest animals excitedly laid out a course that ran for a long distance through the woods, across a large, sunny meadow and up the great hill to the finish line at the top.

The next morning at six, the race began. The big gray rabbit took off like a shot, while old Mr. Turtle slowly pulled away from the starting line. Mr. Rabbit ran and ran and ran. Feeling very sure of himself, he decided that he really didn't need to put forth so much effort. He could see that Mr. Turtle was very far behind. Feeling quite sleepy from all that running, Mr. Rabbit decided to take a little nap. He found a comfortable spot in the soft green grass and went sound asleep.

Mr. Turtle, who didn't feel the least bit sleepy, just kept trudging along, putting one foot in front the other. As the morning wore on, Mr. Rabbit slept and slept, while Mr. Turtle got closer and closer to the finish line. Mr. Turtle went through the woods, across the sunny meadow and up the hill. He didn't stop to rest or play, but kept his mind on finishing the race.

Suddenly, back in the woods, the big gray rabbit woke with a start and was alarmed to see old Mr. Turtle slowly approaching the finish line. Mr. Rabbit jumped to his feet and went dashing off just as fast as his legs would go. His feet were flying and his mouth, gasping for air, was wide open. He desperately wanted to win the race, but try as he might, he had slept too long. In the end he just wasn't fast enough to beat old Mr. Turtle across the finish line.

"Hurrah!" shouted all the forest animals as old Mr. Turtle crossed the finish line just ahead of the big gray rabbit.

That night, there was a big celebration in the forest as all the animals thanked old Mr. Turtle for proving that slow and steady can win the race.

The Importance of Being on Time

One way to help develop children's sense of responsibility to others is to discuss the importance of being on time. In this activity the children discuss the concept of time and the importance of being on time, and draw pictures or write stories about time.

Objectives

The children will:
- explain the purpose of clocks and other timepieces.
- show and state the hours at which they do different activities.
- describe times when they were late and the consequences.
- state the importance of being on time.

Materials

a real or toy clock with moveable hands or a paper-plate clock (directions provided); drawing materials

Procedure

Ask for a show of hands from the children who wear a watch or know someone who wears a watch. Ask them why people wear watches, and why most rooms in offices and homes have clocks. Through discussion, make these points:

- Watches, clocks, and digital time displays tell us the time of day.
- We need to know the time of day because we use the 24-hour "clock" to organize our lives. We go to school at certain times, eat at certain times, sleep at certain times, etc.
- Other people depend on us to be on time for our activities and appointments.

Talk to the children about the importance of being on time. Ask them to talk about times when they were late, what happened, and how people who were waiting felt or how they felt when they had to wait for someone who was late.

Cooperating with Others

Use a clock with moveable hands (or make a clock with the directions below)as a visual aid during the class discussion. This is especially important for young children who may not yet know how to tell time. This, then, also becomes a lesson in how to tell time. Place the hands of the clock to show different times that things happen each day, such as when school begins, lunch time, and when after-school begins. Ask the children to show the time they go to bed, the time of their favorite TV show, and the time they get up in the morning.

After the discussion, have the children draw a picture or write a story about a real or imaginary incident in which they were late. When they finish, have them share their pictures or stories with the rest of the group.

Discussion Questions

1. What would happen if every member of a soccer team showed up for practice at a different time?
2. What would happen if the school bus driver arrived at the kids' bus stops at a different time each day?
3. What would happen if your parents were late to work most days?
4. Who decides what time you have dinner? ... see the doctor? ... go to a movie?
5. Do you get to decide what time to do certain things? What things?

Directions for Making a Paper-Plate Clock

Materials – paper plate, paper fastener, marking pen, and 1 sheet of heavy construction paper

Write the hours with a marking pen around the outside edge of the paper plate. Cut out big and little hands from construction paper. Attach one end of each hand to the center of the paper plate with a single fastener. Make sure that the holes in the hands are large enough to enable the hands to rotate around the fastener.

Creating a Newsletter

When children work together to write and publish a class newsletter they are learning team building and cooperative skills. They also get to express their creativity and develop their writing abilities while they enhance their attachment to their after-school group. The newsletter can also be used to inform parents of the activities and lessons their children are experiencing through attendance in your after-school program.

Objectives:

The Children Will:
- write or dictate stories about their after-school experience
- illustrate the stories with drawings and photographs
- work cooperatively with classmates to produce a product

Materials:

for traditional newsletters: two or three large sheets of heavy paper, writing materials, art materials, camera, and glue.

for a computer-generated newsletter: one or more computers, publishing software, photo-editing software, printer, paper, and a camera.

Procedure:

Tell the children that together you are all going to be working on a class newsletter. Begin by asking questions that will help the children identify what they would like included in the newsletter. Make a list of all their suggestions on the board. Use the question prompts below as a way to engage the children in thinking about what they would like to include. Ask any questions that you think of as well.

- What have you been working on that you would like to include in a newsletter?

- What is the most interesting thing you have learned so far this year?

- What would you like your parents to know about what happened in our after-school program today? This week? This month? This year?

- How can we let our parents know about any problems we faced and how we found solutions to those problems?

In addition to the ideas the children come up with think through class activities and experiences to see if there is anything you might like to suggest for the newsletter.

Once the children, and you, have come up with ideas for what to include in the newsletter have them work in small groups to develop and write the articles. From the list on the board have each group select one (or more) of the ideas that they identified and write an article for the newsletter. Encourage the children to make the entries personal by including quotes from the children and specific anecdotes from the class' day-to-day achievements. Include your comments as well so the parents can see what the children have accomplished both academically and socially. Be sure to ask the children to include illustrations where appropriate.

If you are working with young children you can have the children dictate their stories to you and they can draw pictures to accompany the stories. With the young children most likely you will need to organize and prepare the newsletter yourself. But older children should be responsible for writing, illustrating, and producing the newsletter themselves.

To make a traditional newsletter, create a layout on a sheet of sturdy paper. Draw columns and create a name for your newsletter to put in the masthead area at the top. (i.e. Our After-School Newsletter, or Elm Street After-School Newsletter). When the children have completed their articles either copy these directly into the columns or do the finished writing on separate sheets of paper and glue them within the columns. Be sure there is room to include the children's illustrations. Photos may also be taken and glued in place.

To make a digital newspaper, select a template from the publishing program and follow the directions. If you have multiple computers, divide up the work between teams of children. Take digital photographs and edit them with the photo-editing program. Have the children illustrate some of the stories and scan their illustrations. Clip art can also be used to illustrate some of the stories.

Make copies of the newsletter for each child to take home to his or her parents so they can see how the after-school program operates.

Update the newsletter regularly to continually keep parents current with the class's progress.

Discussion Questions

1. What does it take to produce a newsletter?
2. How must we work together as a team in order to achieve our goals?
3. Is there anything we need to do to improve our teamwork before the next issue of our newsletter?
4. What job would you like to have on the next newsletter, that you haven't already done?
5. Which one of the jobs you worked on did you like best? Why?

Solving Problems and Making Decisions

Decisions, Decisions, Decisions

In this activity the children learn about the importance of making thoughtful decisions by, first, discussing common decision-making mistakes and then writing about some of their recent decisions.

Objectives

The children will:
- describe decisions they have made.
- identify common decision-making mistakes.
- distinguish between difficult and easy decisions, and between important and unimportant decisions.

Materials

one copy of the activity sheet, *I Decided to...,* for each child

Procedure

Talk to the children about how decisions are made. Emphasize that decisions never just "happen," and when someone asks you why you have done a particular thing, it's hardly ever true that you "don't know."

Talk about some common mistakes children and adults make when making decisions. List them on the board.
- doing the easiest thing
- doing what your friend or group does, without thinking about it
- doing whatever will get you into the least trouble
- doing something because it's fun, even though it is not safe or smart

Distribute the activity sheets and go over the directions. Allow the children time to complete the sheet on their own. Circulate and assist non-readers by having them tell you what they did while you record the information.

After the children have completed the sheet, ask each child to share what they wrote and talk to them about some of their decisions. Use the discussion questions that follow and any of your own to prompt thought and discussion.

Discussion Questions

1. Was this a hard or an easy decision to make?
2. If it was hard, what made it difficult?
3. What other choices did you have on this decision?
4. Did you do what people who care about you would want you to do? Why or why not?
5. What was the most important decision you made? What made it important?

I Decided to...

What decisions did you make today? Look at each category below and think about the decisions you made in each. Sometimes you may not even be aware that you are deciding to do something, but if you think carefully you may see that you've made more decision about your life than you realize.

By doing these things, I decided to Take Care of Myself

_____
_____
_____

These are the Safety Rules I followed

_____
_____
_____

This is how I showed I can Get Along with Others

_____
_____
_____

Now, think about playtime or recess. What did you decide to do?

_____
_____
_____

Some of your decisions were easy. You didn't have to think about them very much. Put an "E" beside the decisions that were easy.

Other decisions were more important. Maybe you had to think hard about them. Put a "T" beside decisions you had to think about.

Making Decisions

Learning how to make sound decisions is an important life skill. After a discussion about decision making, the children learn a simple five-step process to use when needing to make decisions.

Objectives

The children will:
- explain how decisions are made.
- apply a decision-making process.
- judge the importance of sample decisions.

Materials

Procedure

Talk to the children about decision making. Explain that each of us makes decisions every day. We decide what to feel, think, say, and do. Often we have several alternatives to choose from when we make a decision. For example, we can wear blue socks, brown socks, white socks, or no socks at all. We can say something nice to a person, or something rude, or sassy, or remain silent. Decision making is about making choices.

Point out that some decisions are more important that others. For example, things that affect health and safety are always important. Such decisions include whether and how often to brush your teeth, saying no to a stranger who offers you a ride, telling someone when you don't feel well, and deciding never to smoke.

Write the five questions from the Decision-Making Process on the next page on the board and discuss each one with the children. Explain that by answering these questions carefully when they have a decision to make, they can usually make good a decision.

Decision-making Process

1. What is this decision about? (definition)
2. Is this decision important?
3. What are my choices? (alternatives)
4. What might happen if I make each choice? (consequences)
5. What would people who care about me want me to do?

Read the following scenarios aloud. After each one, ask the children to decide what is the best thing to do. Call on volunteers and facilitate discussion.

- You miss the school bus. Your parents have already gone to work. Decide what to do.

- You and a friend are walking home from school. It starts to rain hard. A man who you don't know very well offers you a ride in his car. What do you do?

- You are home alone. You promised to finish your homework before watching TV, but a program you really like is starting right away. Decide what to do.

- Your mother tells you not to take your new game to school. You take it anyway, without telling her. It disappears. Decide what to do.

Discussion Questions

1. Which decision was the most important? Which was the least important? Why?
2. How can you figure out your choices?
3. What would happen if you put off making a decision in each of these examples?

Creative Problem Solving

Problem-solving activities provide children with the opportunity to consider the consequences of different decisions thereby increasing the likelihood of making sound decisions in real life. In this activity the children think of alternative solutions to common problems, discuss the alternatives, and choose the best solution.

Objectives

The children will:
- generate alternative solutions to problems.
- evaluate alternative solutions.
- choose solutions from among alternatives.

Materials

Procedure

Announce that the class is going to work together to figure out the best solutions to several problems. One at a time, describe each of the "Solve the Problem" situations on the next page and ask the children what they could do in that situation. Encourage them to be creative and think of many different possibilities. Help them to realize that many problems have more than one possible solution.

Facilitate discussion throughout the problem-solving exercise by asking some or all of the discussion questions during each situation as the children are suggesting possible solutions.

Discussion Questions

1. What might happen if you choose this solution?
2. What makes this solution better than the others?
3. Which of these solutions might make the problem worse?
4. What should you do if you are in danger?
5. If other people are part of the problem, should you ask them to help solve it? Why or why not?

Solve the Problem

- Your mother says you can't have any cookies, but you want some.
- Your mother says you can't have any cookies, but you sneak into the kitchen and get some anyway. In the process you drop the cookie jar and it breaks.
- Your grandmother goes to the store and tells you not to answer the door while she is gone. Someone comes and bangs on the door and then keeps ringing the doorbell.
- Your father goes next door, but says he will be right back. He tells you to stay in the house. While he is gone, a fire starts in the kitchen.
- You want to play with a toy someone else is playing with.
- Someone is standing in your way on the sidewalk and won't let you pass.
- A friend is telling you something, but you can't hear everything he or she says.
- You bump into someone, and the person gets mad, even though it was an accident.
- Your sister takes one of your toys and won't return it.
- The food you want is on the other side of the table, and you can't reach it.
- Someone knocks down the fancy skyscraper you have been building with blocks.
- An older student offers you a cigarette. You are afraid of the student.
- Your best friend borrows and loses your favorite DVD.
- Your little brother or sister is afraid of the dark and always gets in bed with you, which makes it hard for you to sleep.

A Decision-Making Maze

In this decision-making activity the children complete a maze, making healthy choices along the way, and compare the experience to decision making.

Objectives

The children will:
- distinguish between healthy and unhealthy choices.
- compare decision making to navigating a maze.
- choose from among several alternatives.

Materials

one copy of the activity sheet, *Taking the Right Path,* for each child

Procedure

Ask the children to tell you what a maze is. Explain that a maze is a confusing network of paths, some of which lead to dead ends. A maze is a type of puzzle. You have to look at it closely and follow each path with your eye to determine if it leads where you want to go.

Compare decision-making to a maze. Point out that decisions, like mazes, involve many choices, or paths. Some appear to lead in the right direction, but end abruptly or double back. Others lead only to trouble. However, somewhere in the maze, if you study it carefully, you will find the right path. The same is true of most decisions.

Distribute the experience sheets and go over the directions. Tell the children to study the maze to find a path that goes all the way from the beginning to the end. Instruct them to use a pencil to trace the path they take, whether it turns out to be right or wrong. Tell them that they will probably run into some choices along the way. The choices are represented by pictures. Tell them to circle the healthy choices and draw an **X** through the unhealthy choices.

As an extension for older children, have them design their own mazes which also include pictures of safe and unsafe choices. When the children finish creating their mazes, have them exchange them with another child. Each child will then follow the path in the maze they've exchanged.

Give the children a few minutes to complete the maze. Circulate and provide assistance. When the children have completed the puzzle, facilitate a discussion about the experience.

Discussion Questions

1. Which choices did you cross out? Which did you circle?
2. How many tries did you make before you found the right path?
3. Have you ever made a decision that felt like a maze? What was it?
4. When you make the wrong choice on the maze, do you quit or backtrack and try again?
5. When you make the wrong choice on a decision, do you quit or try again? Why?

Taking the Right Path

You will make many decisions as you go through life. Some of the most important involve caring for your body. As you find a path through the maze, you will come across pictures of healthy and unhealthy choices.

Put an **X** over the things that are bad for you.
Put ◯ around the things that are good for you.

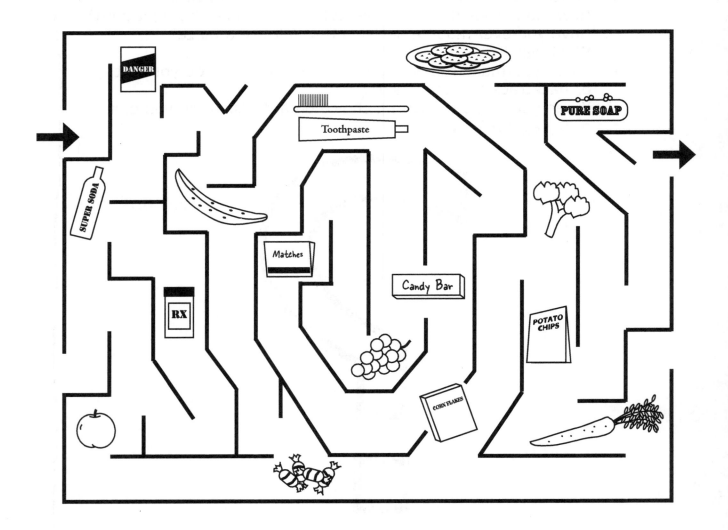

Solving Problems and Making Decisions

My Health and Safety

Making a First-Aid Kit

This activity helps children understand how to treat minor scrapes and bruises in the proper way and the importance of having first-aid items on hand.

Objectives

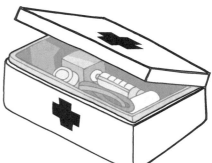

The children will:
- identify first-aid items and their uses.
- help assemble a first-aid kit for the room.

Materials

shoe box (or similar-size container), glue, paint, assorted first-aid supplies (bandages, gauze, tape, scissors, tweezers, cotton balls, antiseptic lotion or gel, antibiotic cream, etc.)

Procedure

Ask the children to help you make a first-aid kit to keep in the classroom. Show them the materials. Hold up each first-aid supply and ask the children to identify it. Discuss the types of conditions or injuries for which the item is used, and the proper way to apply it.

Appoint two or three children to paint the box. Help them print "First Aid Kit" on the lid. Have other children organize the supplies in the box. Ask another group to discuss and recommend a location for the first-aid kit.

Extension

Have the children make first-aid kits to take home. Have them bring in shoe boxes and supplies (or provide the supplies yourself and divide them among the children). Send a note home to parents explaining that the children have made first-aid kits for their after-school class, and now they will be making one to take home. Suggest that the parents hold a family discussion to talk about the kit and a good place to keep it.

Discussion Questions

1. What other items could we put in our first-aid kit?
2. What should you do before handling clean bandages?
3. What should you do to a skinned knee or other wound before covering it with a band aid?

Wash Your Hands

The children learn about the importance of cleanliness through the practice or pantomime of hand-washing and discuss the importance of this ritual in their daily lives. They complete the activity by drawing pictures of dirty and clean hands.

Objectives

The children will:
- practice thoroughly washing their hands.
- understand the importance of hand-washing to maintaining good health.

Materials

hand soap, sink or wash basin, and water; drawing paper and colored marking pens or crayons

Procedure

Ask the children to name times during the day when it is important for them to wash their hands, such as before eating or touching food, after playing outside, before setting the table, and after using the toilet.

Discuss the fact that hand-washing is important not only because it removes dirt, but because it destroys germs that might cause illness. Emphasize that cold and flu viruses are often spread from the hands of the infected person to other people and objects. Frequent hand-washing is one of the best ways to avoid catching colds and flu.

Ask the children to get together with a partner and examine each other's hands. Tell them to notice all of the crevices where germs can hide, such as between fingers, in the knuckles, and under the nails.

If a sink or wash station is available, demonstrate good hand-washing technique. If it is not available, pantomime the process of working up a lather and using one hand to rub the soap around and into the other hand. Have a volunteer sing "Happy Birthday" while you wash your hands (or go through the motions). Explain that singing this song all the way through while you wash is a popular way to ensure that you wash long enough to get rid of germs and dirt.

Have the pairs take turns at the sink, with first one, then the other, washing while the partner sings. Or have all of the pairs work at once, pantomiming the process.

Finally, have the pairs draw pictures of dirty and clean hands by tracing around each other's hands and decorating one of the illustrated hands with "dirt" in the form of smudge marks, pictures of bugs, etc., while making the other bright and clean-looking. When they finish their pictures, have the children show their pictures and tell about them. Complete the activity by leading a discussion.

Discussion Questions

1. When do you wash your hands at home? ...at school? ...at after-school?
2. What is your favorite kind of soap?
3. What should you do if the soap is missing or all gone? (Rub your hands together well as this is the action the kills germs.)
4. What is the most important reason to remember to wash your hands?
5. When should you remember to wash your hands?

Cover Your Mouth and Nose

In this health-awareness activity the children use spray bottles to simulate what happens when they sneeze or cough, and discuss the importance of covering their mouths and noses to prevent the spread of germs.

Objectives:

The children will:
- understand how germs are spread by sneezing and coughing.
- demonstrate how covering the mouth and nose can prevent the spread of germs.

Materials

three or four spray bottles filled with water, dark-colored construction paper (one small sheet per child), paper towels

Procedure

Ask the children to explain how colds are spread from person to person. Call on volunteers. Clarify that colds are spread primarily by touching things that an infected person has also touched, and by breathing germs sprayed into the air when an infected person coughs or sneezes.

Ask the children what they should do when they cough or sneeze. Have the volunteers who identify the following measures stand and demonstrate them.
- turn away
- cover the mouth (or mouth and nose) with a hand
- cover the mouth (or mouth and nose) with a tissue

Hold up a sheet of construction paper and, using one of the spray bottles, spray water onto the paper so that the individual droplets darken the paper. Explain that this is similar to what happens when a person sneezes or coughs. The force of the sneeze or cough launches a spray of saliva and germs into the air. If the person has a cold, anyone standing nearby is likely to breathe in some of the fine spray and may become infected.

Next, turn the sheet over and repeat the demonstration, except this time put your hand or a tissue in front of the spray nozzle so that most or all of the spray is prevented from hitting the paper. Explain that this is what happens when you cover your mouth and nose before sneezing or coughing.

Have the children form pairs. Distribute the construction paper and paper towels (for drying hands). Pass around the spray bottles and have the pairs work together to perform the same experiments.

Discussion Questions

1. What should you do after you sneeze or cough into your hand?
2. What are some other ways in which colds are spread?
3. What else can you do to avoid catching colds? (Wash your hands.)

Stay Healthy

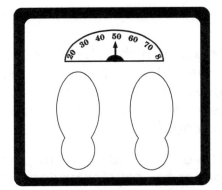

This activity helps the children develop the understanding that they can do many things on a regular basis to stay healthy

Objectives

The children will:
- name specific habits and practices that contribute to good health.
- picture themselves engaging in one or more good health practices.

Materials

drawing materials

Procedure

Ask the children to describe things they regularly do that contribute to their own health and wellness. Call on volunteers and list specific practices on the board. Be sure to contribute things that you do for yourself, too. Add important items that are not mentioned. List such things as:

- eat fresh fruits and vegetables daily
- limit sweets, soft drinks, and junk foods
- exercise
- brush and floss teeth
- get plenty of sleep
- dress warmly when it's cold
- wash hands often
- shower or bathe regularly
- visit the doctor and dentist for checkups
- avoid people who are sick

Discuss each item on the list. For example, ask the children to name the fruits and vegetables they have eaten in the last two days, and have them figure out the number of hours they slept the previous night. Talk about how each item contributes to good health.

Distribute the drawing materials. Have the children draw pictures of themselves engaging in one or more good health practices. Suggest that they select items from the list on the board. Circulate and assist, using the time to further discussion. Have the children share their pictures with the group and then display the pictures around the room.

Discussion Questions

1. What other foods are good for you besides fruits and vegetables?
2. How often do you visit the doctor? ...the dentist?
3. Why is exercise important?
4. What makes people gain weight?
5. How can you avoid getting fat?
6. What is a good health habit that you have that you want to keep your whole life?

Decoding Danger

This activity helps children learn the important safety practice of avoiding dangerous situations by looking at a variety of empty containers and identifying and discussing those that normally contain hazardous products.

Objectives

The children will:
- differentiate between hazardous and nonhazardous products.
- discuss safe behavior around hazardous products.
- learn good safety habits.

Materials

empty bottles and containers for a variety of products, some dangerous and some that are healthy

Procedure

Create a display of containers. Line them up on a table or counter top. Mix the containers of hazardous products with "safe" products. Suggested items:

bleach	prescription medicine
first-aid cream	milk
glue	peanut butter
iodine	pickles
fertilizer	cookies
aspirin	crackers
wine	soda
cigarettes	cleaning fluid
detergent	ink
candy	cough syrup
canned vegetables	bleach

Call on volunteers to come forward and choose an item. Ask the child whether the item is safe or dangerous. If it is a borderline item, discuss circumstances under which it might be dangerous. Talk about the safe handling of dangerous products. Have the children read labels aloud (or read them to the class). Discuss the meaning of various warnings. If the item is safe to use, talk about what it is used for. If it is a food item, discuss what constitutes an appropriate serving. (For example, while soda is not dangerous, drinking nothing but sodas can be bad for your health.)

Use the questions below and you own questions to stimulate thought and discussion.

Discussion Questions

1. Where do you normally find this item?
2. Who uses this item in your home?
3. What should you do if you are not sure about the safety of a product?

My Name and Address

Being able to accurately give someone your name and address in an emergency is important – especially for young children. In this activity the children practice giving their names and addresses while playing an identification game.

Objectives

The children will:
- recite their full names and addresses.
- understand the importance of knowing vital information about themselves.

Materials

full names and addresses of all of the children; drawing paper and crayons or colored marking pens

Procedure

Talk with the children about the importance of being able to provide their full names and addresses, particularly in emergency situations. Go around the room and have each child recite his or her full name and address by saying, "My name is _____ and I live at _____. Some young children may be unable to provide the information. Assist them as needed. (Make a note of those who may require individual coaching at a later time. In some cases, you may need to ask parents to work with their children at home.)

Distribute the art materials. Have each child draw a picture of his or her house. Across the bottom of the picture, have the child print the address of the house in large letters. Circulate and assist with printing if necessary with young children.

Display the finished drawings on a wall or bulletin board where everyone can see them. One at a time, look at the pictures and ask, "Whose house is this?" Coach the appropriate child to call out, "I live at _____," repeating the address.

Leave the pictures on display and occasionally repeat the identification process of two or three houses chosen at random.

Discussion Questions

1. Why is it important to know your full name and address?
2. When and to whom should you give your name and address?
3. Should you give information to people you don't know? Why or why not?

Dial 911 for Help

In this activity the children discuss and learn how and why to make emergency phone calls by role-play dialing 911 and reporting emergencies.

Objectives

The children will:
- practice using the 911 emergency phone service.
- demonstrate good telephone skills.
- practice responding to specific emergency situations.

Materials:

two or more phones (Cell phones that are no longer in service are excellent for this exercise); list of emergency situations (provided)

Procedure

Talk to the children about what might constitute an emergency. Point out that when people really need help fast they can dial 911.

Using a phone that is turned off or not in service, demonstrate for the children by dialing 911 and reporting an emergency. Model good telephone skills.

Talk with the children about the importance of using good telephone habits, especially if they are providing emergency information over the phone. Stress that the children should:

- speak clearly and loudly enough to be heard.
- keep statements short and to the point.
- stay on the line and be prepared to answer questions.

For young children in particular discuss and demonstrate the correct way to hold a telephone while talking. Two at a time, have the children role-play several emergency situations from the list on the next page. Have one child dial 911 and report the emergency, while the other child listens and asks questions.

Coach the children as necessary so that they model and role play the appropriate way to report emergency situations. After the role play, lead a culminating discussion to further reinforce the children's understanding.

Discussion Questions

1. What emergencies have you actually reported?
2. Why is it important to speak slowly and clearly?
3. Why is it important to make short statements?
4. What should you do if you can't answer a question?
5. Who are you actually calling when you dial 911?

List of Emergency Situations

- You witness an automobile accident.
- A fire breaks out in your kitchen.
- A heavy storm washes out part of the road.
- Two teenagers get into a fight.
- A person is hit by a car.
- Your parent becomes very sick and loses consciousness.
- Someone breaks into your neighbor's house and steals money.
- Some kids are spraying graffiti on a school wall.
- You find a gun under some bushes.

What to Do in an Emergency

Through this activity the children use their problem-solving skills while trying to decide how to handle a variety of emergency situations.

Objectives

The children will:
- describe specific steps to take in hypothetical emergencies.
- discuss alternative ways of handling emergencies.

Materials

Procedure

Explain that you are going to describe several emergency situations and you want the children to think carefully about what they would do in each one. If you think the children are sufficiently mature to work in small groups, allow them to discuss each situation among themselves, come up with a plan, and report it to the entire group. Otherwise, facilitate a group discussion of each emergency and generate a plan for handling each emergency with the entire group of children.

List the plan of action for handling each emergency situation on the board.

Emergency Situations

- You are home alone. A water pipe bursts and is leaking water all over the dining room rug.
- You are taking a walk in the woods along a narrow path. Stretched out ahead of you is a snake.
- You go home after school; nobody is home and you realize you forgot your key.

- You awake in the middle of the night, look out your bedroom window and see flames coming out of your neighbor's house.
- You come home from school and notice that the door is open. Nobody is supposed to be home.
- You and your friend are walking home from school in the rain when someone you don't know offers you a ride.
- You are home alone and a stranger comes to the door.
- You wake up in the middle of the night and hear someone in your back yard.
- You are home alone when you start to feel very sick. Your head aches, your stomach is upset and you have hot and cold chills.
- While you are using the toaster oven, sparks and smoke start to come from the electrical outlet.

Discussion Questions

1. What are some things you can do to stay calm in emergencies?
2. What might happen if you got so upset you couldn't do anything?
3. Who can you go to for help when you are at home?
4. Who can you go to for help when you are on your way to school?
5. Who can you go to for help when you are at the park or playing field?

Who to Ask for Help

In this written exercise, the children learn how to take responsibility for personal safety by selecting people from whom to seek help in specific situations. This helps children understand that there are many people available to help them in a variety of situations

Objectives

The children will:
- describe effective actions in situations where help is needed.
- identify specific helping individuals.

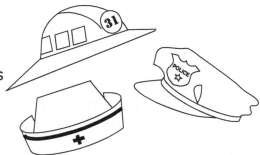

Materials

one copy of the activity sheet, *Ask for Help*, for each child

Procedure

Talk with the children about how to handle problems that are too big or too complicated to solve alone. Suggest that at those times, they need to ask for help. Call on volunteers to describe recent incidents in which they needed to ask for help. Share an incident of your own. Discuss how each incident was handled and brainstorm other actions that could have been taken in that situation.

Distribute the activity sheets. Go over the sheet, explaining how to complete it. Have the children complete the sheet in class. Assist young children by reading over the sheet with them and helping them to write in the answers.

As the children are working, circulate, stopping occasionally to share ideas with the entire class, or allow individual children to share their ideas. Facilitate ongoing discussion throughout the exercise. Have the children take the completed activity sheets home to share them with their parents.

Discussion Questions

1. How do you know when a problem is too big to handle alone?
2. What should you do if the person you would normally ask for help is unavailable?
3. When is it unsafe to solve a problem alone?

Ask for Help

We all have problems at times. You can solve many problems by yourself. Other problems are too big. Sometimes asking for help is the best thing to do. Look at the list of Helpers below and decide who you could ask for help in the situations listed.

Who should you ask for help if...

1. You fall and hurt your knee. _____

2. Your bicycle breaks down. _____

3. Your pet gets lost. _____

4. A stranger follows you to school. _____

5. You have a nightmare. _____

6. You lose your lunch. _____

7. You miss the school bus. _____

8. You feel lonely. _____

9. Your stomach hurts. _____

10. You are worried. _____

Helpers

Mother	Doctor	Friend
Father	Teacher	School nurse or
Principal	Neighbor	health aide
Older brother or	Police officer	Grandparent
sister	School counselor	Religious leader

Sign Language

In this activity the children consider the safety and guidance that signs provide by exploring the school and neighborhood in search of different types of signs, which they identify and discuss. They then make signs for the room.

Objectives

The children will:
- identify different types of signage.
- state the meaning and purpose of traffic and safety signs.
- create useful signs for the classroom.

Materials

poster paper or construction paper; colored marking pens, paints, or crayons

Procedure

Ask the children to recall signs that they have noticed within the last couple of days. Remind them that signs are everywhere—on street corners, curbs, storefronts, doors, windows, utility poles, and many other places. Go around the room and ask volunteers to describe some of the signs they have seen. On the board, list their examples by category. For example, signs that sell something, signs that provide information, traffic signs, and safety signs. Discuss how traffic and safety signs warn of danger, keep traffic running smoothly, and prevent accidents.

Take the children on a walk around the neighborhood and look for signs. Notice the colors and shapes of signs, and read as many as you can. Discuss each sign's value and why it was placed in that particular location. Notice which signs are provided to keep people safe.

As a math extension, have the children keep tallies of the different types of signs and make a chart of results when you are back in the room.

After the walk, place the children into small groups of 3 or 4. Ask each group to talk among themselves and to think of signs that might be helpful in the room. Provide art materials and have the groups create signs for the room. Have the children place them around the room in the locations for which they are designed. Ask each group to explain the reason for their sign.

Discussion Questions

1. What signs do you have in and around your home?
2. Why is it important to obey traffic signs?
3. What signs should you obey when riding your bike, scooter, or skateboard?
4. How do signs help keep us safe?
5. What would happen if there were no traffic signs?

Deep Breathing for Relaxation

Stress is a part of everyone's life—children included. Teaching children strategies for managing the stress and anxiety that they will inevitably face will go a long way in helping them cope with life's challenges. This deep breathing activity is relaxing. Used on a regular basis, it can help ease tensions, anxiety, irritability, muscle tension, and fatigue. Once the children have learned how to do deep breathing, have them use it on a regular basis. Encourage the children to engage in a brief session of deep breathing whenever they feel tense, or anxious, or angry, or upset.

Objectives

The children will:
- learn and practice a relaxation technique.
- understand the benefits of deep breathing.

Procedure

Lead a brief discussion with the children regarding stress and how it feels to them. After identifying some of the negative effects of stress, tension, and anxiety, explain that you are going to teach them a simple breathing exercise they can do anytime to help themselves feel better.

Have the children sit in a comfortable position and close their eyes. Slowly read the following direction:

Inhale and exhale deeply through your nose three times. Place your hand on your stomach just below your ribs. Breathe normally and notice where your breath is. Now take a long, slow breath in until you feel your stomach rise. This is when you know you are doing deep breathing.

Once the children understand the feeling of deep breathing, have them repeat the breathing exercise for several minutes by slowly repeating: Breathe in deeply; hold your breath; slowly exhale through your nose.

If you are working with young children, have them use a soap solution to blow bubbles. This requires nearly the identical breath control as does deep breathing. They learn that slow, steady breathing produces bubbles while hard or soft breathing does not.

Discussion Questions
1. How did it feel to do deep breathing?
2. When can you use deep breathing in your life?

Caring for the Environment

Observe a Tree

This first activity in the environmental unit allows the children to observe and record perceptions of nature in a cooperative learning setting. This whole unit is designed to broaden the understanding of the living world around them so they will become thoughtful decision makers about the wise use of natural resources.

Objectives

The children will:
- observe and describe features of a chosen tree.
- collaborate to graphically express their impressions of the tree.

Materials

one copy of the tree template (provided) for every two children; colored marking pens, paints, or crayons

Procedure

Take the children for a walk to a nearby area where they can see several trees. Have the children select one tree and observe it in detail. Ask them to touch and describe the bark. Pick a leaf and pass it around, noticing its color, texture, size, and shape.

Look at the tree as a whole. Ask the children:
- What does it look like?
- What is the tree's shape?
- How tall is it? How wide?

Have the children look at the tree from different angles—standing up, squatting, lying on the ground. Discuss their observations.

When you return to the room, divide the children into pairs and provide each pair with a copy of the tree outline. Have the pairs work together to embellish their trees, making their illustrated tree look as much as possible like the real one they observed on the walk. Have the pairs share their completed drawings with the class. Ask them to describe how the tree looked to them. Make notes on the board.

Extension

On a second walk, allow the children to choose one tree to "adopt." Spend some time at the tree. Notice what it looks like, take a measurement of its diameter, make bark rubbings, pick leaves off the ground and bring them back to the room. Have the children do a computer search to identify the scientific and popular names of their adopted tree. Have them draw and label pictures of the tree. Return to the tree regularly.

Discussion Questions

1. What was it like to work together on the same drawing?
2. How did you make decisions about what colors to use and how to draw the tree?
3. What did you see by closely observing the tree that you have never noticed before?

Our Need for Plants

The children discuss the mutually beneficial relationship between people and plants, and talk about how various plants are beneficial and necessary to humans and the balance of nature.

Objectives

The children will:
- describe how people depend on plants, and how plant life benefits from people.
- identify specific uses for a variety of plants.

Materials

pictures or photos of a variety of plants

Procedure

Begin by discussing how Earth's plants and animals contribute to the balance of nature. Explain that each type of plant has a job to do, and all things in the environment are connected in important ways. Brainstorm examples of these mutual benefits, including:

- Plants absorb the carbon dioxide that humans and animals breathe into the atmosphere.
- Humans breathe the oxygen that plants return to the atmosphere.
- Many plants provide food for us to eat, such as fruits, vegetables, and grains.
- Trees and other plants are turned into lumber and other building materials.
- Plants provide cooling shade.
- People cultivate plants and create new varieties.
- People feed plants and make them healthier.
- Plants make our gardens and yards beautiful.
- Through science, people develop products that reduce and eliminate plant diseases and pests.

Ask the children to name things that plants need to be healthy, such as sun, water, soil, nutrients, and air. Then ask them to name things that people need to be healthy, such as food, water, air, and shelter. As the children suggest items, create two lists on the board and compare them. Discuss the similarities and differences.

One at a time, hold up the plant pictures and ask the children to name some ways in which people might use each plant. Have the children identify the broad category to which each plant belongs, including trees, flowers, and shrubs.

Discussion Questions

1. Why do so few trees grow in the desert?
2. What happens to your house plants when you forget to water them?
3. What is the name of the type of store that sells plants?
4. What types of plants grow in your yard?
5. Why is it important to human beings to take good care of the plants around them?

Plant a Seedling

The children plant tree seedlings and begin to care for them. This is an excellent activity to coincide with National Arbor Day, the last Friday in April.

Objectives

The children will:
- plant and care for seedling trees.
- identify and provide for plant needs.

Materials

a tree seedling for each child, plus some extras (they can be ordered from the *National Arbor Day Foundation: www.arborday.org* or phone 888-448-7337), potting soil, and paper cups

Procedure

Announce that the children are going to plant seedlings, care for them in class, and then take them home and transplant them into their own yards. (Children who do not have yards may be able to donate their seedlings to their school or give them to relatives or other children.)

Show the children pictures of the types of trees whose seedlings you are providing. Discuss what each type of tree needs in the way of care.

For young children write each child's name on a paper cup, and carefully punch two or three small holes in the bottom of each cup (older children can do this for themselves). Distribute the cups and soil. Then assist each child to choose a seedling and plant it.

Place the planted seedlings in trays or on plates to collect drainage. Arrange them in a sunny place and have the children water them as needed. Encourage the children to notice any growth or changes.

After caring for the plants for a while, encourage the children to take their seedlings home and replant them.

Discussion Questions

1. What are some ways in which we use trees?
2. Why is it important to take good care of trees?
3. When people cut down trees in the forest, what can they do about replacing them?
4. What kinds of trees grow in your neighborhood? ... in your yard?
5. What is your favorite kind of tree?

Taking a Nature Walk

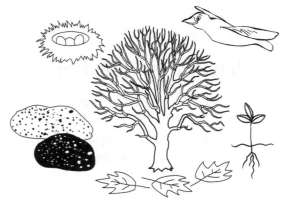

In this art and nature activity the children collect objects on a nature walk and use them as the basis of craft projects.

Objectives

The children will:
- identify a variety of natural items.
- collect samples, discuss them, and use them in displays.

Materials

art materials required for the craft projects of your choosing (see below)

Procedure

Take the children on a walk through the neighborhood. If possible, walk through a park, field, or wooded area. Along the way, observe nature. Encourage the children to pay attention to what they see and hear: busy insects, singing birds, the breeze moving the leaves.

Bring along a shopping bag and, while walking, ask the children to look for samples that can be taken back to the room without disturbing the natural environment. Try to collect the following:

- petals
- leaves
- bark
- twigs
- stems
- soil
- pods
- fronds and thorns
- feathers
- nests
- bones
- shells
- grass
- branches
- stones
- wild flowers

Have the children use the samples from nature in one or more of these craft projects:

Mobiles

Suspend a selection of compatible objects from a branch with string cut to various lengths.

Pictures

Have each child select one sample. Help the children glue their items to pieces of construction paper. Then have them draw or paint other details around the objects, completing pictures. For example, they might start with a leaf and draw a tree around it. Or start with a feather and draw a bird around it.

Display of pressed flowers

Press flowers and leaves between two sheets of waxed paper placed between the pages of a heavy book. When pressed and dry, name and label the items and make a bulletin-board display, or glue the pressed flowers and leaves to the front of folded construction paper to make cards.

Scene-in-a-box

Using an old shoe box, create a miniature nature environment. Place the box on its side so that the opening is in front. Then arrange soil and several objects inside the box, creating a scene.

Spray of branches

Tie several branches together with an attractive ribbon, adding other items, such as acorns. If you like, spray paint the branches first. Hang the arrangement on a door or wall.

Color cards

Have the children sort the samples from nature by color, putting all the greens, browns, reds, and yellows together. Encourage the children to notice the variations within each color group. Make "color cards" by printing "Brown like a ..." or "Green like a ..." on the top of a large piece of card stock. Then glue selected items of that color to the card. Display the cards around the room.

Discussion Questions

1. What was your favorite part of the nature walk?
2. What did you see that you've never noticed before?
3. How many animals did you see? What were they?
4. What kinds of insects did you see?
5. What was the most interesting sound you heard on the walk? What made the sound?

Tending a Mold Garden

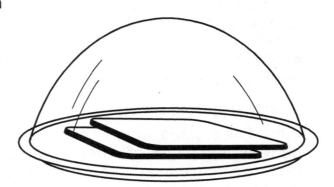

In this science activity the children discuss the benefits and uses of molds, and then experiment with growing and observing mold on bread.

Objectives

The children will:
- observe and describe the growth of mold on bread.
- review some of the environmental and scientific uses of molds.

Materials

bread slices, one or more plates, glass jars or bowls large enough to invert over the bread slices to create see-through covers, magnifying glass

Procedure

Ask the children if they have ever seen moldy bread or fruit. Call on volunteers to describe what the mold looked like.

Discuss the benefits produced by molds in nature, and positive uses of mold in science:

- Molds cause the decomposition (breaking down) of organic material, releasing and recycling nutrients.
- Molds are used to make cheese, soy sauce, certain kinds of teas and sausages, and other foods and beverages.
- Molds are used to make citric acid, an ingredient in many foods and beverages.
- The "wonder drug" penicillin is made from mold.

Explain that the class is going to start a mold garden and watch the mold grow.

Have the children moisten a slice of bread with water and place it on a plate. Make sure the bread is damp but not soggy. After about an hour, have the children cover the plate with the glass jar and place it in a dark place. Repeat the process with additional bread slices (from different types of bread) if you wish to conduct experiments and observe if mold looks/grows differently on different kinds of bread..

Look at the bread daily. When grey or blue patches appear, mold has begun to grow. Allow the children to use the magnifying glass to examine the mold more closely. Each day, observe and discuss the changes in the growth of the mold. Have the children keep a daily observation journal of the changes they observe.

Discussion Questions

1. How does the bread mold look the same or different from other molds you have seen?
2. How long was it before the bread mold was first visible?
3. When was the mold first visible through the magnifying glass?
4. Have you, or a member of your family, ever been given penicillin? How did it work?

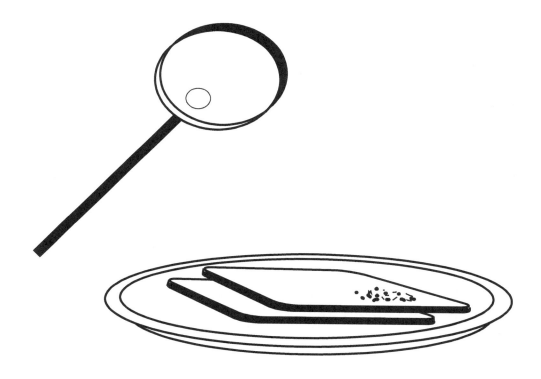

Learning About Organic Gardening

This science experiment shows the children how to build and maintain a mini-compost pile and then use the soil for planting. The experiment continues as the children observe and record the growth of bean seeds in the soil they have made.

Objectives

The children will:
- explain how compost is made.
- tend and observe a small amount of compost as it breaks down into soil.
- use the newly created soil to grow a plant.

Materials

a large can or jar; assorted organic waste materials, such as coffee grounds, fruit rinds and skins, dried leaves, grass, crushed cereal, all broken into *very small* pieces; bean seeds, styrofoam cups with 2-3 small holes punched in the bottoms

Procedure

Discuss with the children the elements that plants must have to grow—sunlight, air, water, nutrients, and soil. Explain that the soil provides support for the plant as well as storing moisture and nutrients.

Talk about the difference between healthy, well-nourished soil and poor soil in which plants do not grow healthy and strong. Talk about how farmers keep their soil healthy.

Point out that many people and organizations make compost for their yards and gardens. Explain that the benefits of using compost are twofold: compost builds healthy, rich soil while providing a means for recycling organic waste. If computers are available, have the children do research on the benefits of organic gardening.

Have the children layer the composting materials into the jar or can. Have them stir the mixture and moisten it with water. Cover the container and punch several small holes in the top. Place the container in a warm location and look at the contents daily. Every few days, have the children stir the mixture. When everyone agrees that the mixture has turned to soil, have the children use the soil to plant bean seeds.

For the second part of this activity you may want to provide additional potting soil beyond what was "created" by the children. This way each child can grow his or her own seed. If the children are each growing their own plant, have them put their names on their styrofoam cups.

Have the children fill their cups about 3/4 full of soil. Then place a bean seed on top and add another 1/2-inch of soil and water gently. Place the cups in a sunny location and have the children water their cups regularly to keep the soil evenly moist (not soggy) while the seeds germinate. Observe the cups daily.

Have the children keep a record of how many days to germination, and then the growth of the bean plants.

When the bean plants are large enough, plant them in a outdoor garden area, if available, or else the children can take their plants home.

Extension

Provide a variety of dried beans and seeds, as well as glue and heavy paper or cardboard. Have the children draw pictures and then "paint" the picture by gluing the beans and seeds onto the surface of the drawings. Preserve the pictures with a clear plastic spray or a light coat of shellac.

Discussion Questions

1. How does the compost container feel to the touch?
2. How does the compost smell?
3. How is this soil the same or different from the soil in your garden at home?
4. What do you notice about the bean plants as they grow?

Pet Rocks

This is a good activity to help children to be observant of the natural world and to sharpen the children's appreciation of texture, shape, and color in natural objects and also to make them aware that similar objects in nature have individual characteristics.

Objectives

The children will:
- describe the characteristics of individual rocks.
- identify the similarities and differences between rocks.

Materials

dishpan, mild liquid soap, one or more scrub brushes, paper towels, magnifying glass, sandpaper

Procedure

Ask the children to look at different rocks around their homes, neighborhoods, at school, and at the after-school site. Instruct them to each select one rock that they particularly like and bring it to after-school.

Ask the children to examine their rocks carefully. Tell them to notice the shape, color, texture, and weight. Call on a few volunteers to describe their rocks to the group.

Fill the dishpan with soapy water and place it on a table along with the scrub brushes. Have the children take turns scrubbing and drying their rocks. Ask them to examine the rocks again and notice any differences created by cleaning the rocks. Call on volunteers to describe those differences. Encourage the children to examine their rocks using the magnifying glass. Facilitate discussion throughout this process.

Write each child's name on a piece of masking tape and attach it to his or her rock. Display the rocks together on a table.

Have the children write or dictate paragraphs describing their rocks. Display these near the rocks.

Discussion Questions

1. What colors do you see in your rock?
2. How does your rock feel to the touch?
3. How is your rock the same as someone else's? How is it different?
4. What does your rock have that none of the others have?

Learning About Our Feathered Friends

After examining books and pictures featuring birds, the children construct a bird house and bird models.

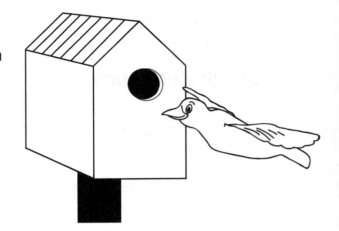

Objectives

The children will:
- identify different kinds of birds.
- notice similarities and differences between birds.
- construct models of birds for a display.

Materials

pictures of birds, books featuring birds, bird feathers, and a nest (if available); cardboard box, glue, masking tape, scissors, construction paper, clear plastic tape, crayons, or colored marking pens; light colored construction-paper cutouts of birds (template provided)

Procedure

Create a display of bird pictures, books, and other objects. Invite the children to join you in examining and discussing the items.

Play the following simple game with the children: make statements about birds and other animals, such as, "It has feathers," "It has four legs," "It has a beak," and "It says meow, etc." Have the children call out, "It's a bird!" after any statement that describes a bird.

With the children's help, make a birdhouse from the cardboard box. Glue the pieces together and cut out a small, round door. Allow the children to decorate the birdhouse with marking pens.

Using copies of the bird template, make paper models of birds. Follow the instructions included with the template to cut out, fold, and tape the pieces together. Allow older children to do their own cutting and assembly. Assist younger ones. Allow the children to color and decorate their birds in any way they wish. Suggest that they get ideas from the bird books and pictures.

Display the birdhouse and paper birds on a table, or hang them from the ceiling or a shelf. If the children want to place the birdhouse outside, weatherproof the exterior with a heavy coat of shellac.

When you have finished with the bird display, the children can take their birds home as a gift for a family member on a special occasion

Discussion Questions

1. Which of the pictured birds have you actually seen?
2. What bird names do you know? Have you seen those birds?
3. What is the name of the bird that you made and colored?
4. What do you like best about birds?

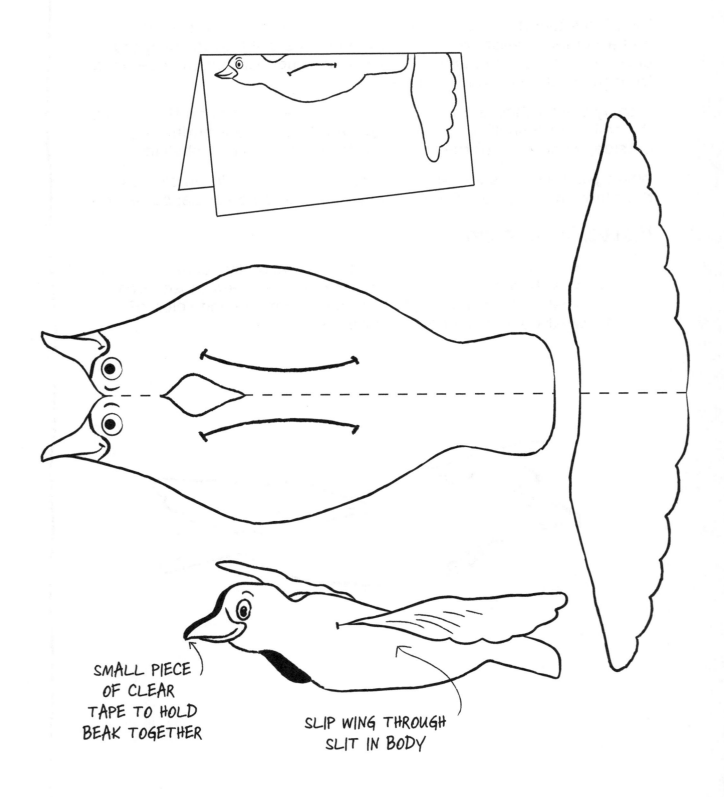

SMALL PIECE
OF CLEAR
TAPE TO HOLD
BEAK TOGETHER

SLIP WING THROUGH
SLIT IN BODY

Experiments with a Pinwheel

In this science experiment the children construct pinwheels and use them to observe and learn about air currents in different locations and circumstances.

Objectives

The children will:
- construct a pinwheel.
- describe how the pinwheel is affected by different air currents.

Materials

one copy of the pinwheel (template provided) for each child, plastic drinking straws, straight pins, small beads with holes, tape, and crayons

Procedure

Talk with the children about the air that surrounds them. Point out that although air is hardly noticeable, it carries the oxygen that we must breathe to stay alive. Explain that the wind is the movement of air, and that storms involve the movement of air masses across regions, bringing rain and snow.

Demonstrate the movement of air by constructing pinwheels and observing them move in response to air currents.

Distribute the unfolded pinwheel patterns, along with the other materials. Have the children color their patterns on both sides and cut them out. Demonstrate making diagonal cuts from the corners. Caution the children not to cut on the dotted lines.

Following the directions provided with the template, help the children fold and tape the corners, push a pin through the center, through a single bead, and through the end of a plastic straw.

Caution: Using pliers, bend the end of the pin down until it lies flat against the straw. Then tape the end of the straw, completely covering the end of the pin.

Have the children experiment with their pinwheels. Ask them to find out what happens when they blow on the front, the back, and the sides. Hold the pinwheels in front of air conditioning or heating vents, and open windows. Take the pinwheels outside and have the children use them to judge how fast the wind is blowing.

Discussion Questions

1. What are some other things that move and turn in the wind?
2. What do the trees do in the wind?
3. When were your pinwheels completely still?
4. When did they move fastest?

Caring for the Environment

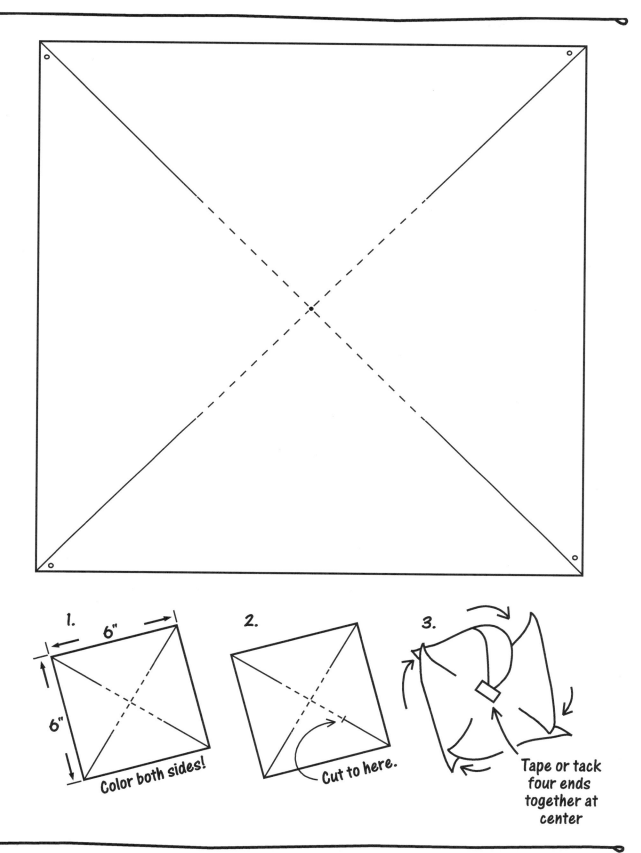

1.

6"

6"

Color both sides!

2.

Cut to here.

3.

Tape or tack
four ends
together at
center

Learning About Recycling

The children discuss the benefits of recycling and learn what kinds of items may be recycled in their community. This series of activities on recycling and litter control teaches the children the importance of preserving and improving the environment and how they can participate in caring for the earth.

Objectives

The children will:
- define recycle and distinguish it from reuse.
- identify items that are recycled.
- describe the benefits of recycling.

Materials

items that are recycled in your community (check your local waste hauler's web site); for example, newspaper, glass jar, aluminum can, plastic bottle, mixed paper, corrugated box, and grass clippings

Procedure

Help the children become aware of the importance of recycling. Display a collection of recyclable items and ask the children what they have in common. Call on volunteers and give the children time to consider a number of possibilities. If no one gives the answer you are looking for, explain that all of the items may be recycled in your community.

Discuss the meaning of the term recycle. Explain that recycling is different from reuse. When something is reused, it does not change form. A reused coat is still a coat. A reused door is still a door. But when something is recycled, it loses its form and the material from which it is made is used to make something new. For example, old newspapers may become greeting cards, grass clippings may be composted into soil, and cement walkways may become new roads or freeways.

Point out the following benefits of recycling:

- Recycling saves space. When items are recycled, fewer discards end up in crowded landfills.
- Recycling saves energy. Less energy is required to recycle (melt aluminum cans, crush glass) than to make new products from raw materials.
- Recycling saves resources. When we recycle, old materials are made into new products, so fewer raw materials are used.
- Recycling reduces air and water pollution caused by manufacturing.
- Recycling encourages innovation and creates jobs as new products are developed.

Discussion Questions

1. What items does your family recycle?
2. What is recycled at your school? ...at our after-school site?
3. Why is it everyone's responsibility to recycle?

Litter Lookout

In this science and math activity the children collect data on the prevalence of litter in designated locations and create anti-littering posters and then conduct research to determine the environmental impact of litter.

Objectives

The children will:
- define litter and explain why it is undesirable.
- observe how much litter collects in specific locations over a period of one week or more.
- create posters encouraging people not to litter.

Materials

large sheets of poster paper and colored marking pens, paints, or crayons

Procedure

Ask the children to define the term *litter*. Help them understand that litter is any item that has been improperly discarded. For example, a scrap of paper is not litter if it is thrown in a trash basket or recycling container. However, if it is dropped on the floor or the street, it becomes litter.

Discuss the reasons that litter is bad for the environment. Mention that it takes away from the beauty of the landscape and can cause illness and injury to pets, wildlife, and humans.

For one week have the children keep records of all the litter they notice in places like the school grounds, parks, the playground, the neighborhood, city streets, and their own yards. Make a class "litter chart" with columns for locations such as those mentioned above. Each day, put tally marks under the headings where the children have spotted litter.

Distribute the art materials. Have the children work in small groups to create anti-litter posters. Have each small group explain their finished poster to the larger group then display them around the room.

When the children have finished their posters, have them research the answers to these questions:

1. Each person in the United States uses about 580 pounds of paper a year. In one year, what is the total amount of paper used in the United States?
2. Each year 25 billion Styrofoam cups are thrown away. If all of these cups were placed end to end in a line, how many times would the line circle the earth?

Discussion Questions

1. Which location that we observed collected the most litter? Which collected the least?
2. What kinds of litter did you see?
3. What ideas do you have for reducing the litter in these places?
4. Why do people throw trash on the ground?
5. When was the last time you littered? Why did you do it?
6. Where does much of the trash that people drop on the streets come from?
7. What can you do to reduce litter in your neighborhood?

LITTER WE HAVE SEEN THIS WEEK

DAY	PARK	PLAY GROUND	SCHOOL	CITY STREETS	OUR NEIGHBORHOOD	OTHER
Monday	✔✔✔	✔✔	✔✔	✔✔✔	✔	✔✔
Tuesday	✔	✔✔✔	✔✔✔✔	✔	✔✔	✔
Wednesday	✔✔✔✔✔	✔	✔✔✔✔	✔✔✔	✔✔✔✔	
Thursday	✔	✔	✔✔	✔✔	✔	✔✔✔
Friday	✔✔	✔✔	✔	✔	✔✔	✔
TOTALS	**12**	**9**	**13**	**10**	**10**	**7**

Environmental Scrapbook

In this collaborative activity the children create a scrapbook of news articles, stories, and other items pertaining to the environment.

Objectives

The children will:
- identify and collect articles and other items about the environment.
- organize and present the materials by subject matter, in scrapbook form.

Materials

a large scrapbook, tape or glue, and samples of articles, charts, pictures, other items concerning environmental issues, and items from nature to embellish the scrapbook

Procedure

Show the children the scrapbook. Announce that the class will collect interesting items on the environment and put them in the scrapbook. Suggest that the children look for magazine and newspaper articles, download and print articles, graphs and charts from the Internet, and collect photographs and pictures. Have the children create poetry, drawings, and stories to include in the scrap book as well as being sure to include good news about the environment along with problems. List possible subject areas, including:

- endangered species
- air and water pollution
- preservation of parks and open spaces
- destruction of rain forests
- oil spills
- effects of population growth
- recycling and reuse
- global warming

As the children bring in items, discuss each one with the class before placing it in the scrapbook.

Have the children sort, arrange, and paste the items into the scrapbook, adding headings and captions. Have them use items from nature such as pressed leaves and flowers to enhance the visual appeal of the scrapbook.

Encourage the children to share their environmental scrapbooks with parents and other visitors to the class. As they tell about the items they have included, it reinforces their environmental learnings.

Discussion Questions

1. Which item that we've included in our scrapbook did you find most interesting?
2. What did you learn from the item?
3. What ideas have you gotten for things that you can do to help the environment?
4. What do you think is the most serious environmental problem we have, based on the articles and information we collected?

If your heart is in Social-Emotional Learning, visit us online.

Come see us at
www.InnerchoicePublishing.com

Our web site gives you a look at all our other Social-Emotional Learning-based books, free activities, articles, research, and learning and teaching strategies. Every week you'll get a new Sharing Circle topic and lesson.

 INNERCHOICE Publishing
15079 Oak Chase Court
Wellington, FL 33414

Made in United States
Troutdale, OR
10/30/2024

24313068R00091